Outstanding shop designs

Outstanding shop designs

THE ARTS OF THE HABITAT

Series directed by Olivier Boissière

Front cover
Shoebaloo Shoeshop,
Amsterdam, The Netherlands.

Back cover
Dr. Baeltz, Tokyo, Japan.

Preceding page
The varied contrast between
the forms, materials and colors
creates here the right
conditions to whet the desire
of the customer for the objects.

Publisher editor: Jean-François Gonthier
Art director: Bruno Leprince
Cover design: Daniel Guerrier
Editing staff: Olivier Boissière, Olivier de Vleeschouwer, François Roux
Translation: Rubye Monet
Assistant to the publisher: Sophie-Charlotte Legendre
Correction and revision: Françoise Derray, Jack Monet
Composition: Graffic, Paris
Filmsetting: Compo Rive Gauche, Paris
Lithography: ARCO Editorial, Barcelone

This edition copyright © TELLERI, PARIS 1998
All illustrations copyright © ARCO Editorial except for page 6 and the cover
ISBN : 2-7450-0016-0
Printed in Italy

Contents

Introduction

Ever since Boucicaut and his like invented the modern department store that promised the "Bonheur des Dames," the retail trade has been involved in a long love affair with architecture. For it is clear that the enticement of the customer and the repetition of the act of purchase depend largely on the setting. Since the second half of the 19th century, department stores have borne the mark of some of the most talented architects of their time—from the Bon Marché of Boileau and Eiffel to Innovation of Horta, from the Harrods of Stevens & Hunt to the Schenken of Mendelsohn, architects have raised remarkable structures, novel creations in the urban landscape, many of which have stood the test of time.

It is quite different for the smaller stores and shops whose lesser size and lower cost caused them to become quickly obsolete. Some exist today only in memory, others in faded photos—a Viennese tailor's shop designed by the dandy Adolf Loos, a delightful perfume shop of Süe and Mare, an automobile showroom by Mallet Stevens. Few have survived, yet it is surprising that we have even as many as we do, for their lives are like those of fragile fireflies that light up and vanish with every passing mode and trend. The constant renewal of the merchandise and its appearance requires a parallel renewal of the decor.

The eagerness to remain in fashion inevitably evokes the stubborn and insoluble question: in the art of enticing the customer, which is paramount, the product or its setting?

On the whole, though, the guidelines that the retail shop designer must follow are simple ones, based on space needed for display, storage and trying or testing of the merchandise as well as paying for it. In addition there are the considerations (not negligible, it is true) of lighting and security.

The ideal, of course, always pursued and never attained, is that both in succession—the setting first, the product afterward—should add to the attraction and not interfere with each other.

The stores and shops presented in this work offer a panorama of enticing settings whose brightly-colored fantasy or stark hieratic aura reflect the manners and morals of our time.

Their locations are eclectic, their geographic spread covers the planet. The voyage of their discovery takes the reader from Iceland to Spain, from Japan to the United States, stopping on the way in France, Britain, the Netherlands, Germany and Italy. May we express the hope that, after closing this book, the potential shopper will also have had a taste of delectable sites.

Tempus Expeditions,
San Diego,
United States
The spectacle
is permanent and the
clothing tells a story.

Thierry Mugler
Paris, France

For a fashion designer, a shop on the Avenue Montaigne is a tangible sign of success. An address on this elegant thoroughfare near the Champs-Elysées is also a good way of putting oneself in the path of the cosmopolitan clientele who haunt the nearby luxury hotels. Space available on the Avenue is at a premium. The site occupied by the firm of Thierry Mugler has a banal facade barely marked by two little posts, a glass door, four mannequins in the window, and the designer's signature as a shop sign. Nothing prepares you for the spectacle inside.

Architect Patrick Philippi has done a remarkable job with what is hardly more than a long narrow corridor. One side is a smooth wall covered on the lower part with satin-finish metal and on the upper part with frosted glass. The other side has a series of niches separated by shiny metal buttresses highlighted by bands of stainless steel. In these niches articles of clothing and accessories are displayed ever so discreetly—mystery, stealth, concealment are but another strategy of desire. At the rear of the corridor, the space grows wider and leads to the fitting rooms, tall cylinders with narrow horizontal slits and lighting that emanates strangely from below. The floors are uniformly covered with a speckled resin in a neutral beige color. But the transcendent feature of it all is the ceiling. Its stunning curves and countercurves, its smooth lines tinged electric blue by the indirect lighting, float overhead like solid clouds studded with starlike points of light. Like a space age reinterpretation of Finnish designer Alvar Aalto.

We already knew the designer's weakness for all things military—epaulettes and gold braid—and his amused fascination for a certain imagery not far removed from socialist realism. Here he invites us to voyage in the dream universe of Space Wars. A war without victims, of course, except for those who fall into the thrall of fashion...

Starry lights on galactic blue: the long corridor stretches into the distance like a passage to a parallel universe.

From the street, the shop hides its charms and masks its mystery. The intentionally ordinary shopfront gives no hint of the surprises that await within the gates.

Opposite:
Enigmatic mannequins stand like sentinels organizing the space. Their gestures seem to beckon toward a fabulous fashion world.

The double ceiling
suggests the infinite
space of an interplanetary
voyage. The sinuous
forms, like star-studded
clouds, stand out
against the strange clarity
of a luminous sky.

In the wall niches, the
presentation of clothing
and accessories is given
a dramatic touch by
indirect lighting reflected
off the metal walls.

The cylindrical fitting
rooms, lit from below,
resemble some space age
sarcophagus. Or is it a
magic cubicle where
wondrous transformations
are performed?

Opposite:
View of the section
devoted to men's fashion.

12 Thierry Mugler, Paris, France

Opposite:

The women's dressing room, like the rest of the shop, is bare of all anecdotal adornment. The dramatic effects come from the light. Blue light from fluorescent ceiling tubes gives an unreal quality while the indirect lighting of a little corner table adds a note of comfort and intimacy.

View down the corridor toward the shop entrance and the four mannequins in the window, reflected in the long wall mirror.

Floor plan showing the distribution of the different spaces.

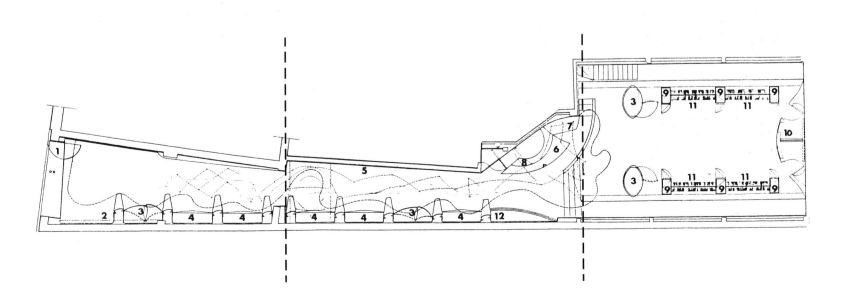

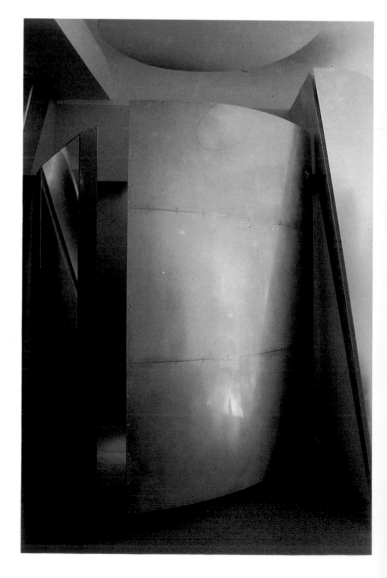

14 Thierry Mugler, Paris, France

Detail of display shelf with hats
and other accessories.

Opposite:
The try-on cabins seen
from various angles, inside and out.

A monolith of absolute simplicity: a
counter in the shape of an elliptical arc.

The broad central aisle with its original red brick vaulted ceiling
retains the proportions of the former structure. Pale walls
and floor create a luminous background against which the clothing
on display stands out. Discretion is also present in the uniformly
slender lines of the furniture and display racks.
The only theatrical feature are two large pivoting screens covered
with transparent nylon, which extend from floor to ceiling
and seem to filter the whole perspective.

A series of small intimate spaces, intended for negotiation, reflection or relaxation. The materials are simple, painted metal and concrete, and the colors natural, white walls, pale green beams, ivory tiling and couches in warm brown.

Maurizio Peregalli

Kenzo

Milan, Italy

Italian design owes a great part of its vitality to the sporadic emergence of a number of anti-establishment movements coming from young and undisciplined groups. In the mid-1980s this role of protest and provocation was filled by a turbulent little group assembled around Maurizio Peregalli under the somewhat immodest name of Zeus. Zeus set itself up in Milan, outside the usual circuits, near the Porta Genova in the old quarter of the Navigli still humming with craft workshops. With manifestoes, exhibitions and lots of juvenile uproar, Zeus wanted to abolish categories in design, mixing together products and furniture, architecture and fashion. Maurizio Peregalli came to be the favorite designer of Armani, for whom he designed a series of boutiques in the major capitals.

When Kenzo, the most Parisian of Japanese designers, arrived to open his showroom in Milan, it was Peregalli he came to, certain that he would bring to the project a shared vision and a cultural bridge.

A designer's showroom is at one and the same time a display area, a workshop, a space in which to receive distributors and retailers and a point of direct sales. It is not a shop in the traditional sense of the word and its space must allow for a certain informal freedom of movement as well as for some more private areas where business is done and deals are closed.

Peregalli found himself here with a raw industrial space, spacious and with a good height. He kept the great central aisle and the brick vaulting, one of the most common features of turn-of-the-century industrial architecture, as well as the skeleton of an old freight elevator which today, well-scrubbed and prominently displayed, has acquired the status of an archeological artifact. The lateral spaces open directly on this aisle and a gallery distributes to the mezzanine another series of offices and workshops. Here Peregalli uses simple materials of Italian rationalist architecture of the moment: gray concrete breezeblocks, painted metal structures and staircases whose metal steps are softened by a supple covering. Pivoting partitions the whole height of the aisle filter the overall vision with their shimmering reflection. Beige tile floors and walls give the ensemble a pleasant brightness and provide a neutral background to highlight the few garments displayed, which add a bright touch of color. The furniture was chosen in the same spirit and gives the space a feel that is both discreet and reassuring. The ambience of the Kenzo showroom is one of serenity and quiet activity that goes so well with the image of the creator.

The main reception area
at the front of the shop:
the blond wood of the
ceilings lends warmth
and a pleasant feeling
of comfort. It is repeated
in the borders of the
sliding doors, which
can be opened or closed
to modify perspectives.

In the rear, a precise
and functional area
that serves as both office
and workshop.

Left, one of the staircases
leading to the mezzanine
gallery where offices
and workshops are
situated. Right, the space
where the collections
are shown, with a saffron-
yellow ramp perched on
broad black wood steps.

Floor plan
of the premises.

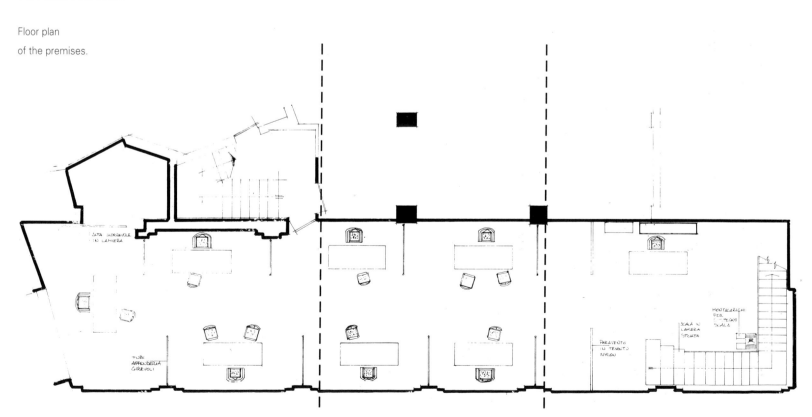

Metal staircases leading to the mezzanine underscore the character of the spaces they serve. In the reception rooms, the silhouette of the steps against the white breezeblocks forms a diagonal pattern. Or they define an alcove by a subtle play of harmonies and reflections—the colored surface of the furniture is doubled in the mirror, where the staircase and its twin meet to form a step pyramid. At one end of the central aisle the inner workings of an old freight elevator stand guard at the foot of the stairs in a composition like an industrial landscape.

Josep Font
Barcelona, Spain

In the central room, with
its pebbled floor,
the ornamentation is
deliberately understated,
reduced to a mere
whisper: white walls with
a few scattered starfish
shapes, simple forged iron
for the rack, the chair
and the naive decorative
flower.

Opposite:
Through the plate glass
facade, the whole shop
is visible to the eye.
Seen from the street,
the interior takes
on the function of a shop
window.

Josep Font and his partner Luz Diaz belong to the young generation of Catalan fashion designers who came to the fore-front in the 1980s. They acquired international fame in the salons of Paris and Milan, then decided, like a number of their peers, to open shops that would be permanent showplaces for their creations. It was naturally in their home port of Barcelona that they anchored their first showroom, a place of modest dimensions but an admirable location on the famous Paseo de Gracia.

From the architecture of clothing to that of interiors the boundary is thin and eminently crossable. The two accomplices decided to put all their know-how into designing a space that would accurately reflect their image.

Located on the ground floor of a small nondescript building, the shop facade was not very promising. They opened it up completely and put a plate glass window across the whole width, which enables one to see at a glance all that is inside. The space is divided into three overlapping areas, a main room fronting on the street, a central room like a little courtyard and a small mezzanine. The passage from one space to another is marked by small understated signs: a cement vault encrusted

On the mezzanine,
the space is focused
around two elements:
the large screen
of wrinkled linen
and the original wooden
structure overhead,
where theatrical lighting
highlights the
"archeological" details.

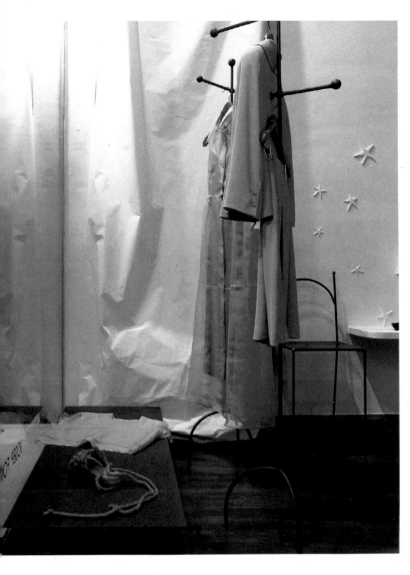

Both the window decoration and the clothing display
are reduced to their simplest possible expression.
A low table holds some accessories and a wrought iron
rack has two garments hanging from its slender twig-like
rods. To add relief and offset the rigor of the rest,
a large roll of crumpled paper seems to detach itself
from the wall and cascade over the floor.

The central room is treated as a sort of patio. The single
flower in its pot, the lighting of the niche and fitting room
(visible on the right) are enough to evoke the play of sun
and shade of a little interior garden.

The commercial aspect of the premises has been
intentionally eclipsed. All that suggests the selling function
are three small wall shelves and a glass table
on two wrought iron tripods, one shaped like a star,
the other like a crescent moon.

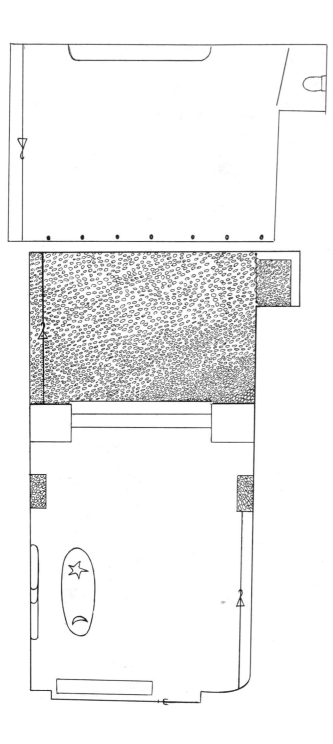

with small flat stones, a change in flooring, passing from the dark parquet of one area to a polished pebbly concrete that evokes a riverbed. A dark wood staircase leading to the mezzanine has a banister and railing reduced to their simplest possible expression: a thin line of wrought iron with a gentle curved (a fleeting allusion to Mannerist curves?). The backdrop consists of uniformly white walls with delicate markings in the shape of a starfish and a ceiling that keeps its original beams. The merchandise itself takes up little space: simple bars fixed to the wall and holding ordinary polished wood hangers relegate it to the periphery of the space, except for one perched on a metal stalk and exhibiting a single garment in the middle of the window. The furniture too is reduced to its simplest expression: slim metal chairs, a table with a slender base and a simple glass tabletop. Two little niches in the rear wall, an artificial flower, a screen of deeply wrinkled white linen, an unfurled roll of paper in the palest of pastels, imperceptible lighting—decidedly, it is a theatrical composition in a minor key, a minimalistic vision. To make a final point—as if disdaining commerce—there is no counter and no cash register. The key words that sum up Josep Font's Barcelona showroom are: economy of means in the service of implacable elegance.

Plan showing the distribution of three interconnecting spaces: the front room, pebbled surface central space and the mezzanine.

From the mezzanine, a view of the main room separated from the rest of the shop by a broad cement vault inlaid with small flat stones.

Brown parquet stairs
lead to the mezzanine,
whose protruding floor
is supported by a simple
white column.

Detail of the access
to the mezzanine from
the staircase. The handrail
is a plain wrought iron rod
ending with a small ball.

The mezzanine is
protected by a line of
sinuous iron stalks, each
one topped with a golden
ball.

Opposite:
A glimpse of the Paseo
de Gracia over the
guardrail and through the
stone-encrusted archway.

A multifunctional space where the convivial bar area, with its bistro tables and chairs, is just next to the display racks. It is multi-temporal as well, with contemporary elements mingling with vestiges of bygone days. The large clock placed amid the piles of clothing recalls the passage of time, or perhaps, on the contrary, a complete stopping of time in this strange setting where all is anachronism.

Opposite:
In the central zone, varied materials and decorative features are superimposed. A "new-age" concrete sofa with a split back and a pocked and pitted slab for the seat, a table made from an old conveyor belt, useless bones of old industrial machinery. A strange juxtaposition of striated wood partitions and colored walls lit by a series of glass cylinders. The entire scene is bathed in bluish light from fluorescent tubes in the ceiling, where exposed aeration ducts are also visible.

Joseba Beranoaguirre
Trucco
Bilbao, Spain

The Basque designer Joseba Beranoaguirre is one of the most creative and intuitive interior architects of the Iberian peninsula. At 30 he already had to his credit clothing and footwear stores, driving schools, assorted shops and offices. All these realizations enabled him to affirm a creative talent recognized on an international level.

The Trucco company sells and distributes clothing and shoes. Their Bilbao shop, designed in 1990, followed another project carried out in Madrid for the same firm. The Bilbao one posed all sorts of problems—material and economic ones as well as problems of schedule and specifications. But Beranoaguirre was able to find novel and ingenious solutions while respecting the identifying marks the company had already established in its outlets of Madrid and Pamplona, creating an interior atmosphere based on similar lighting and layout and with repeated use of the company logo.

Along the way, some classic concepts concerning the entrance, shop window and showcases were subjected to an original reinterpretation and some new ideas were introduced into the Spanish commercial landscape—like having a bar inside the shop, not to encourage customers to drink but rather to give their visit an unexpected twist.

Walking through the shop, one grasps at a glance the option chosen by Beranoaguirre: to make each zone easily identifiable—the entrance and the central body devoted to clothing and the other areas (bar, toilets, stock area and shoe store) laid out all around. The spirit of the place is manifest in the design and the lighting.

The entrance is worthy of special mention: a bare space between street and selling area that enables the visitor to see nearly the whole shop at a glance. Eight glass tubes mounted on old pieces of discarded industrial archeology are the only elements here that recall the classic shop window, featuring only a few well-presented objects, two mannequins and a small 18th-century altar of carved oak.

The visitor makes his way deeper into main area of the shop where, with a great simplicity of means, colors, materials and textures combine with deliberately suggestive lighting to create an atmosphere full of tactile imagination. This space is divided into rectangular areas, placed perpendicularly. The first, extending the entrance, is the central core of the shop devoted to ready-made clothing, the second is devoted to shoes.

The area allocated to accessories is centered round a circular counter at the intersection of the two parts of the store. It is made of oxidized iron and antiqued brass plates, with one part covered with glass for the presentation of costume jewelry.

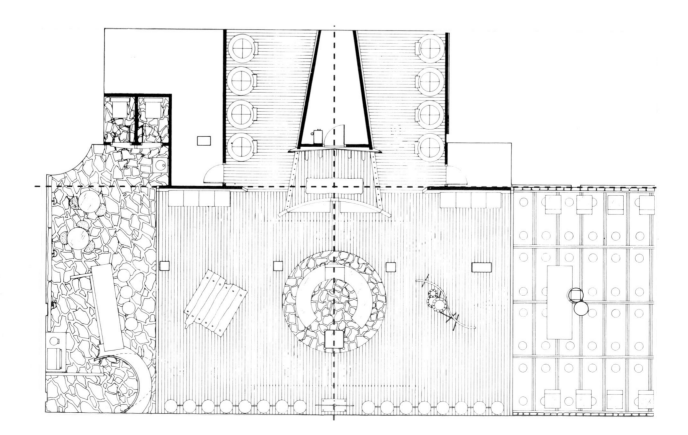

The central counter,
at the intersection of
the two parts of the store,
one for shoes and
the other for clothing,
is a circular structure
made of riveted plates
of iron and brass. One
part is covered with glass
and serves as a display
case for costume jewelry.
Its strategic position
is further highlighted
by the attractive red cupola
with its antique street
lantern from Madrid.

Behind the central
counter, an oddly-shaped
mirror, rather like a ship's
sail, stands against
the back wall, breaking up
the long line of garments.

Opposite:
Another view of the
mirror, here reflecting part
of the counter cupola, the
display racks and the area
of the fittings rooms.

Floor plan showing the
organization of the store.

The ceiling is a fine sienna-colored plaster cupola. The lantern that lights it comes from an antique shop in Madrid and was originally a street lamp. The windows are made of assorted antiques found in attics and demolition sites as well as a sort of stylized form of Beranoaguirre's own making that towers over the central counter.

The air conditioning was an unavoidable necessity and the ceiling was very low. The designer opted for leaving the ducts visible, respecting the overall tonality of the place.

The shoe area is identified by slight changes in level of the floor and direction of the floorboards. On each side of the room are installed the fitting rooms, eight free-standing cylindrical units, with wooden doors of grained oak that are genuine antiques, quality pieces found at a scrap yard.

The craftmanship of the bar is extremely original. The floor and part of the walls are made of quartzite. and the bar itself is an assemblage of fire-resistant bricks and the tables are gears of old conveyor belts. The reserve of the bar is dissimulated behind a concave wall topped by an inverted golden cupola. The sink is a mix of wood, quartzite and Gaudí-inspired ceramics. The key concept is in the indirect lighting from the ceiling, via neons and halogens that enhance the blue tones of the ambience.

Beyond the functional constraints of a complex selling space, the architect has achieved a design that is strong and unusual, a sort of Ali Baba's cave sprinkled with signs of industrial archeology with its useless and rusted machines that evoke the city's bygone days. In a Bilbao in search of a new economic and cultural expansion, Trucco is like a landmark, expressing neither nostalgia nor complacency, destined simply to serve as a basis for the search for a new identity.

On either side of
the circular counter,
in front of the clothing
racks, are two unusual
display units: four-
wheeled carts on which
lie unmatched planks
of wood. Old timbers
from a shipwreck? from
a demolition site? All
conjecture is possible...

Opposite:
Another view of the
central counter and its
reflected image.

The bar where visitors
can have a rest and
a drink is made of fire-
resistant bricks. The floor
and part of the wall
is in quartzite. Behind the
sienna-colored concave
wall topped with a golden
dome is the reserve and
utilities.

Some of the obsolete objects collected here have been given a use, usually off-beat and unpredictable. An ancient bit of plumbing has become a support for the clothing racks. But the antique telephone sits silent, reduced to mere decoration.

Two views of the try-on booths in the back of the store. Eight free-standing cylinders arranged in two groups of four. Each one has been given a sort of slotted conical cap and an antique oak door set in a frame of midnight blue.

Detail of the wooden panels where a rusty chain and frayed rope are used as a decorative element.

Display cases made of glass cubes on bases from old industrial parts. The lighting comes from a delicate network of small halogen lamps.

A streamlined metal wall has a dual function: it holds some objects on display and also separates the store area from the fitting rooms. The separation between the areas is also marked by the change in direction of the floorboards.

General view of the
fitting room area. In the
foreground, a double
structure is used
to display shoes.
On the opposite side,
this structure becomes
a sofa with a little side
table added as a cozy
touch (see page 30).

Sbaiz

Lignano Sabbiadoro, Italy

Opposite:
The central staircase wraps around a rusted metal structure, shaped like a giant ship's prow and whose surface resembles the flank of an old rusted tanker.

The colors and materials blend harmoniously to create a cool nautical atmosphere. White walls—matted finish for the walls, satin for the floors—transparent doors and glass furniture, with a warmer touch added by the blond wood.

The organization of this immense space is through a complex arrangement of uniformly white walls. The theme of the sea (present just nearby) is found in various allusions and decorative details—from behind porthole-like openings, the sources of light have an aquatic cast.

Lignano Sabbiadoro (which means golden sand) is a seaside resort on the bay of Marano, near the Gulf of Venice, whose visitors come largely from nearby Udine. Like many of her sisters on the Adriatic coast, the town suffered the outrages of uncontrolled development in the 1960s. When the chain of ready-to-wear shops Sbaiz Moda decided to create an outlet here, the best it could find was a large empty space in a very ordinary but well-situated building at a corner property on the fine avenue that parallels the sea. The task of designing the interior was given to the Florentine architect Claudio Nardi.

In an Italy where contemporary architecture has to struggle against an omnipresent history, Claudio Nardi found himself in an unusual situation, where the neutrality of the existing space, its very absence of value, gave him a wide margin of freedom. He seized the opportunity to achieve a creation that

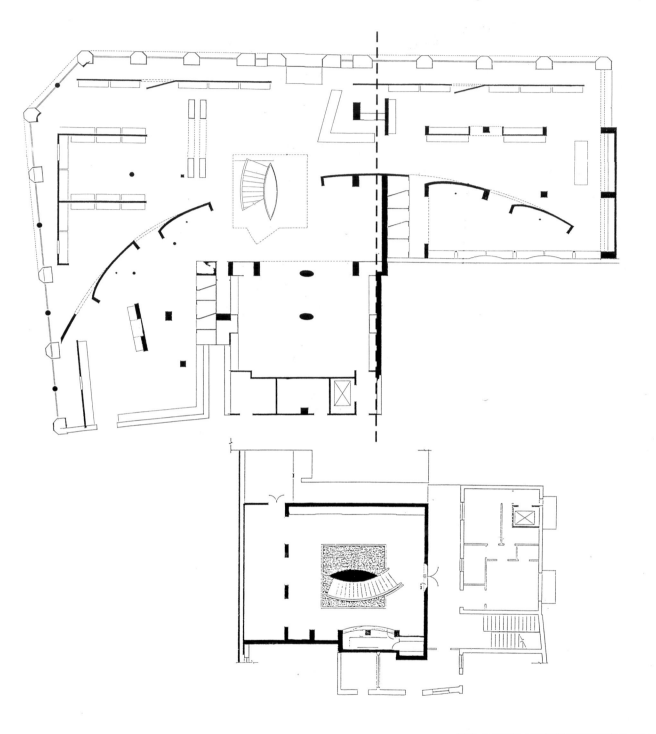

Opposite:
In a whiteness of sea foam animated by curves, friezes of light and flaring, tapering or elliptical columns, one walks through the vast space as through a recomposed city, recognizing streets and squares and perhaps a suggestion of a coliseum dotted with a geometric pattern.

Plan of the building and its organization divided into two levels.

Outside, the shop windows are large glass panes framed in varnished wood, another reference to the world of ships and the sea.

Following pages:
One of the perspectives
from the ground floor
from which we see
the mezzanine and
general view of the
spiral staircase, strategic
point toward which
all else converges.

goes far beyond merely remodeling the premises and redesigning the facade. The underlying thought was to rebuild the image of an exotic palazzo caressed by wind, sun and sea air, a place of tropical inspiration in the manner of those novels which, as Nardi says, "carry you away to distant colonies where shadows filter the rays of sun through blinds and draperies, and cast golden flecks on blond wood and white columns."

The architect's first preoccupation was to create a living connection with the street by lining the facade with a covered arcade broken by a portico of metal posts. In a first allusion to the sea—the structure of the original facade is covered with varnished wood framing large panes of glass that function as shop windows. Inside this admittedly oversized space, Nardi used another urban strategy—creating a path that evokes a little piece of the city with its streets and squares... This device makes use of two distinct forms— the orthogonal grill that corresponds to the geometry of the space and a sweeping curve superimposed upon it. This conceptual setting is given form by white walls, some marked by a rectangular motif, columns that gradually widen to resemble cones, forming capitals at the top, porticoes marking invisible boundaries, a formal and minimal interplay of forms that give the place a scale more in keeping with its commercial vocation. A large spiral staircase winds around a massive volume, profiled like a ship's prow and whose rusty metal looks as if it came from the flank of some old freighter. The furniture is sparse and discreet, the flooring is of clear resin on the ground floor and wood on the upper floor, and the diffuse light aureoles the whole place with its whiteness.

Sbaiz Moda deploys a universe of rounded forms and sharp angles, alternates solids and hollows in an ambience at the edge of unreality.

The try-on booths—garnet-colored pleated velvet, pinched here and there with golden clips—sum up the spirit of The End: elegance with a good dose of theatrics and a pinch of humor. They recall those illusionist acts where the magician led his lovely partner into just such a velvet cage, only to "disappear" her with his magic wand.

Opposite:
The ground floor room presents a monochromatic perspective with a series of blond archways and the bronze tones of the varnished parquet. As a counterpoint, the walls covered with veined marble add a cool and sophisticated note.

Eduard Samsó

The End

Ibiza, Spain

The natives of Ibiza undoubtedly have a hard time recognizing in the space designed by Eduard Samsó the vestiges of the old fishmonger's where they used to come to shop. The site, located in the heart of the old quarter of Ibiza, occupies two levels of a typical fisherman's house and despite its state-of-the-art appearance, The End has not renounced all of its former history. Stone arches inside and unaltered facades outside bear witness to the architect's will not to break completely with a past so rich in memory.

But the circulation of customers cannot remain the same in a fashion boutique as it was amid the dripping vats of a fish market. The prime objective of Eduard Samsó therefore was to totally rethink the space, with an accent on a search for freedom of movement organized around the different areas necessary for the sale of clothing.

The shop is open at both ends, one end on the street, the other on the maritime passage, and offers a long perspective perpendicular to these two busy thoroughfares. This impression of great size is obtained by creating an inner void with five zones of circulation bounded by the four original arches. The staircases, very visible in this configuration, appear as fully-fledged spaces of their own. They rise up spontaneously, as if inviting the visitor to pass from one level to another.

Over the access from the street a golden anagram with the name of the shop. Both entrances, surmounted by balconies, confer, by their form and the choice of materials, a feeling of mass and solidity. The veined marble that covers the walls, floor and ceiling give from the outset the tone of the interior design. The place is resolutely turned toward both refinement and excessiveness, and yields to the temptation of theatricality tinged with humor. A case in point: the try-on booths, three garnet-colored niches that seem to have been left behind after a performance by some mysterious magician.

In the same desire to favor movement and not hamper freedom of access to the different display areas, a unity of color obtains throughout the boutique. Blond parquet flooring, with walls and ceilings in the same shade, open a vast visual perspective, intelligently punctuated by several elements of more sharply contrasted color. This warm and mellow ambience is accented by discreet and cleverly-positioned points of light that define a play of light and shadow. In this deliberately bare space, the display tables mark the boundaries, preventing monotony and emphasizing the roundness of the vaults.

The extreme sobriety of the floors contrasts with a zigzag of metal bars on the ceiling, which support and connect the

The racks and display tables form an alternative to the roundness of the vaults. Perched on tall metal legs, these structures are ever-so-slightly inclined, imparting a feeling of perpetual movement.

try-on booths and create a sense of movement. Other metal tracks hold the lights. Like some metallic magic carpets, folded and floating in air, the staircases are held up by thin metal stalks that add to the feeling of fragility. Their blackness contrasts with the other dominant colors and creates an interrogation, like an echo to the mystery of the three velvet-shrouded booths. An enormous canape of incongruous and old-fashioned charm seems to invite us to have a rest and enjoy a few minutes of people-watching just near the mirror. Where will she come from, the beautiful maiden that appears to look at herself in the mirror? Will she descend the staircase or fly out of the booth like the magicians's pigeon?

Crossing the space from one end to the other, the visitor is overcome by a double feeling. That of solidity, inherited to a great extent from the historic past of the house itself, and the resolutely contemporary idea of great mobility and the perfect accord between aesthetic aspirations and commercial imperatives.

Like the racks and tables,
the display cases are
also inclined, an aesthetic
choice but also
a commercial one.
These treasure chests
that lean forward toward
the customer seem
to promise some
exclusive rights
to their contents.

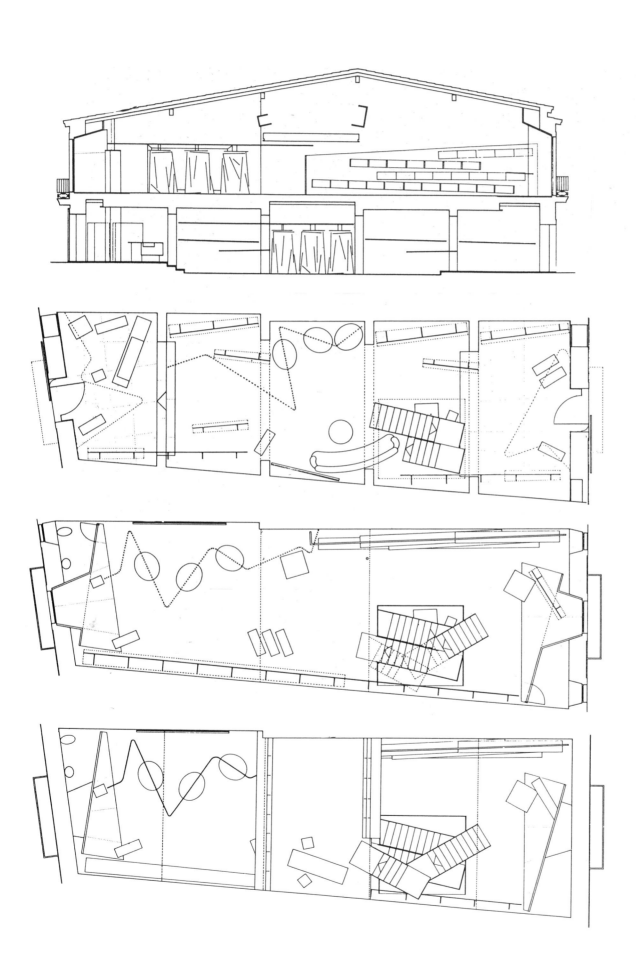

Cross-section of
the building and plans
of the three floors that
compose it.

Opposite:
The black staircase
leading upstairs, in
marked contrast with the
blond wood floors and
pale walls, looks like a
miracle of imbalance. It
rises as if weightless,
deploying a most unlikely
succession of flights
which, at each landing,
seem to break off all
relations with one
another.

Seen from above, the staircase seems
to decompose completely. The steps appear
to pivot and the railing segments interweave
their slender lines in a complex visual network.

Opposite:
The dizzying sensation given by the stairs
contrasts with the promise of comfort offered
by the large upholstered couch situated
just below. The desired effect throughout
this unusual space is to create illusions
and provocations, to tease and to perplex.

Galleri

Reykjavík, Iceland

The shop entrance opens directly into the space of the original establishment. Visible on the right is a part of the large central pillar around which the new arrangement has been organized. The main counter is placed along the side wall of the pillar.

Opposite:

The glass surface of the counter provides a showcase for a collection of ladies' pumps but it has other functions as well. Its boards of fine maple are a vertical restatement of the floorboards, also of the same wood. Aside from its aesthetic qualities, it is a storage unit holding, behind invisible doors, administrative items needed for the shop.

In a time of global networks of communication, insularity has lost its quality of isolation. This may be what Margrét Hardardottir and her partner Steve Christer set out to prove. After completing their studies in the United Kingdom they decided to go back to Iceland and set up shop in Reykjavík. A spectacular and cleverly-conceived house they had built in Germany assured their firm, Studio Granda, a certain interest from the international media. Like some latter-day wandering players, they can practice their art from their far-off island home.

Early on, their work showed a predilection for natural materials, and they keep on using these to good effect. The enlargement of the fashion shop Eva-Galleri is a perfect example of their technique. It also shows that talent does not have to have major projects to assert itself and that strong ideas carried to their conclusion produce original works.

At Galleri a central pillar, independent of the walls but imposing by its color and mass, assures the functional organization and determines the life of the space. The area around it, though

The smooth blue block of the pillar forms the boundary
between the two areas of the shop, a frontier marked
on the floor by a change between maple parquet and basalt
stone. Seen from this angle, the pillar seems massive
and impenetrable, but the impression is contradicted
by the narrow band of light coming from within—behind
the pillar, in fact, are the fitting rooms.

56 Galleri, Reykjavík, Iceland

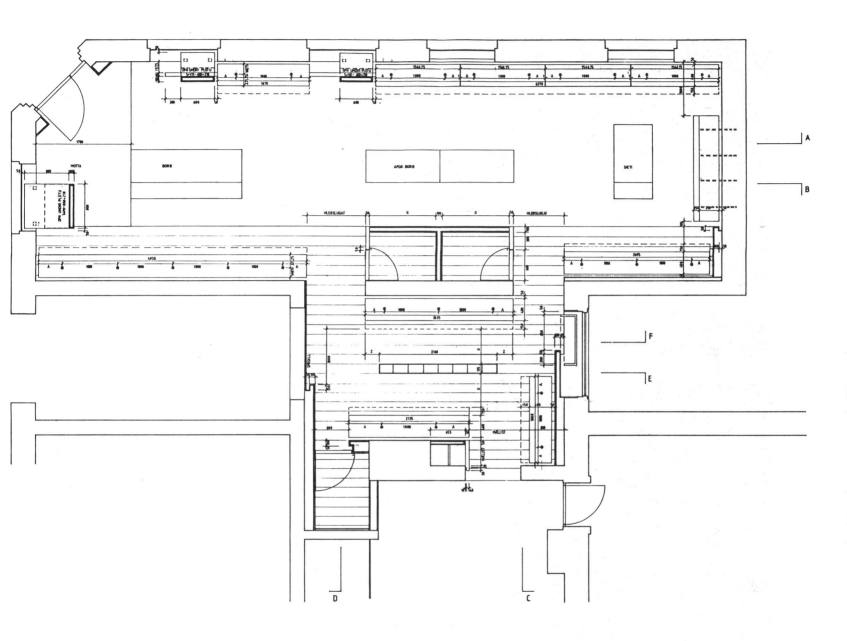

The T-shaped plan
of the shop and another
view of the showcase
and pillar.

View of the passage
linking the old section
with the new.

Opposite:
In the newly-annexed
space, a mirrored wall
reflects the rear of the
central pillar, fitted out
with shelves and a rack.
We can dimly make
out a window framing
the bust of a mannequin.

rather small in size, acquires thanks to this pillar a nearly giratory sense of movement. The project was to combine two shops, Galleri and Eva, into one, incorporating as well a former office situated between them. A new body, joined to the rear of the preexisting rectangle, but of much smaller dimensions (4,5 m x 3 m) made possible the connection between the two shops by means of a passage opened in the wall. The T-shaped area thus obtained increases the circulation inside the shop. The wall with a pillar acts as determining organizing element of the space, both by its central position and its function as a frontier between the old volume and the new.

Access to the shop is through a corner of the original rectangle, which has three outer facades. In addition to its strong color, contrasting with the whitish tones of the walls and ceiling, the central pillar makes its presence felt as a master element. Everything revolves around it. Shelves and clothing hangers are disposed against the perimeter walls. A shelf space has been built against the pillar, facing the new addition and therefore invisible to the entering visitor. For the rest, all the display units work together to further the idea of direct correspondence between the perimeter and the center.

The floor of the original shop is almost entirely covered by maple parquet flooring. A showcase in front of the pillar is made of the same material, which has the effect of linking it to and integrating it with the floor. Aside from its display window, this showcase also has invisible doors behind which are stored files and order books. For the floor of the new section the architects chose a noble basalt. It marks the transition between the spaces and, through its matter, color and natural force, it echoes the power expressed by the central pillar. The changes of material between stone and wood are signaled on the perimeter walls, by recesses and variations in floor plan. A system of grills diffuses warm air by means of an underground heating system.

The three materials, maple, basalt and steel, are again present in the wardrobe elements, assuring the visual unity of the ensemble. This unity is reinforced by a regular and filtered lighting that comes from a series of luminous points embedded in the ceiling and from light tracks placed behind some of the shelves. From the moment they enter, customers are enveloped by the atmosphere of the place, with its pronounced character and natural feel, an atmosphere both sober and elegant, just like the garments it has to offer.

Eva

Reykjavík, Iceland

The empty space that once separated the clothing store Eva from the shop called Company is now occupied by this new edifice. The inserted area is so well-integrated into the existing structure that it feels like its natural extension.

Opposite:

After the glass-covered entrance, the white side wall lowers to align itself with the height of the windows, forming a corridor, from which a staircase bridges the change in level and leads directly to Company area.

In the beginning there was an empty space between the fashion shop Eva and its neighbor, a shop called Company, which was devoted to home decoration. The project entrusted to Studio Granda was to construct a volume between these two buildings, which would occupy the rear of an alley perpendicular to the main street.

The objective was more than just to connect Eva and Company. The architects had to provide a function for the newly-created space and to attract passers-by to this space where they could walk around as in a patio.

Today a rectangular body unites the two shops. On the outside it is half as tall as the highest wall and barely detached from the lowest one. From the inside, however, the height of the room represents half the lowest wall of the courtyard. An inner staircase now links the two boutiques.

Although the length of the patio has been reduced by this new construction, it now seems to extend inside, well beyond the shop window. This effect of continuity is accentuated by the very nature of the shop window, which starts at floor level and is not very high. Lastly, the patio floor, made of granite slabs, is slightly sloping so as to augment the feeling of flow from the outside toward the inside.

Outside, the appearance shows a perfect integration of the new volume between the two original buildings. Neither overshadowed nor too visible, the new facade looks like an obvious and logical extension of the old walls. The two materials that make it up have that purity of form and matter

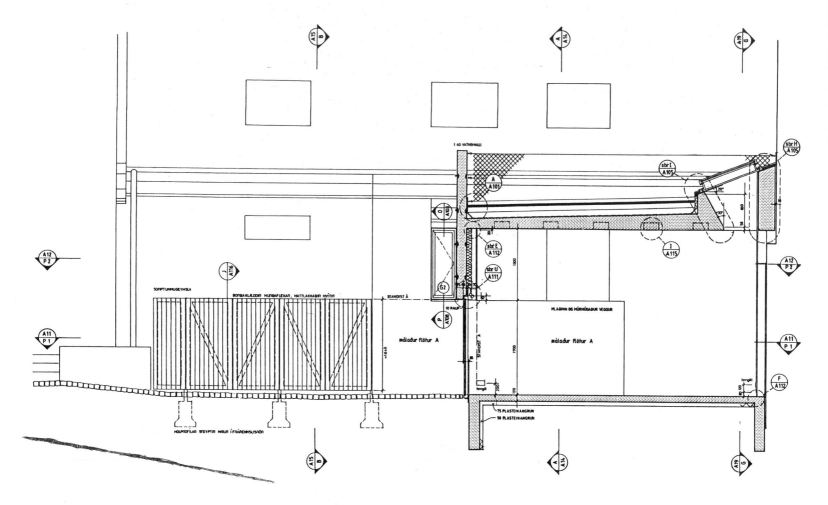

Transverse cross-section of the new edifice.

Opposite:
Through a clever artifice, a segment
of white wall seems to detach itself
from the Company building to penetrate
the new concrete facade. It gives
the impression of interlocking spaces
that communicate from within.

The austerity of the concrete is animated
by four quadrilaterals etched into the facade
on which a series of metal rings forms
a repeating pattern.

so prized by these young Icelandic architects. The upper part, made of concrete, is supported by the white side wall and assures visual unity with the opposite wall. The lower part, all of glass, gives a strange impression of emptiness that attracts the eye, like a door left open at the rear of a courtyard that sets our imagination working. As a shop window, it ideally fulfills its role, catching the attention of pedestrians who pass by in the main street.

To complete the integration, a part of the wall seems to have become detached on the right and embedded itself in the new facade. This visual trick makes us feel that the two volumes also communicate within.

The sobriety we find outside is further echoed within. The space is deliberately austere, both in its forms and in the colors and materials chosen. This absence of fantasy shows a desire to focus rather on the objects displayed which, indeed, stand out forcefully. Set out against the walls, they seem both flexible and fleeting, the very nature of a shop being, of course, to periodically renew the objects it offers for sale.

Between the polished concrete floor and the ceiling made of a mixture of concrete and sand, the gray-white walls form an ideal neutral background for the objects on display in cases of shiny black steel. The lighting, sober and uniform, is a cunning combination of electricity and natural light. The artificial lighting comes from a great number of light wells in the ceiling, which help to alleviate its heaviness. As for the daylight, it enters through the shop window and through a series of windows above the single solid wall, which diffuses a discreet and neutral light.

Functional and efficient, sober but not cold, this new space that has emerged between two existing buildings has quickly found its own identity. A unifying link, it holds a strategic position and plays its role with rare discretion.

A deliberately neutral interior. The muted colors and total absence of anecdotal detail help draw attention to the objects displayed along the walls. The great concrete expanse of the ceiling is lightened by the many circles of light as well as by a series of square openings through which natural light comes in.

Opposite:
The concrete facade is broken by a broad area of glass, level with the street, which serves as both entrance and shop window.

View of the interior and the black steel display units that stand out against the pale gray walls.

Torsten Neeland

Ocky's

Hamburg, Germany

Ever since art broke through the limits of traditional painting and sculpture in which they had developed from the Renaissance on and appropriated for itself the spaces and objects of everyday life, its frontier with the neighboring disciplines of architecture, design and fashion has become a subtle one—basically only a question of intention, as the latter disciplines retain a utilitarian aim that art still denies. Reappropriating the looks and manners of art has become common practice in our consumer society.

This boutique, part of a trendy German fashion chain called Ocky's, is a new example. The young designer Torsten Neeland has created in the suburbs of Hamburg a model of a minimalistic and perfectly-executed selling space.

The references are explicit—to the work of Donald Judd, the American artist who died recently and who had himself forged ahead by applying the mathematical principles of his specific objects to a series of furniture items, and to the work of his friend and accomplice Dan Flavin, whose luminous sculptures are made of fluorescent tubes commonly used for industrial lighting.

It was an exercise fraught with dangers—an old building with no particular virtues, a difficult space, long and narrow, high-ceilinged, fragmented in three parts by two protruding walls, Torsten Neeland has been able to get the most out of it. The shop front follows the opening of the facade, outlined by a simple frame of black brick with the firm's logo in the middle of the window. In the three interior spaces, the architect underscores the elementary geometry—smooth walls, sharp ceiling angles, uniform flooring of gray resin. In this setting he places the display and storage units and the various accessories like pure distinct objects, treating each one with understated precision and technical perfection.

Cantilevered from the wall and with no visible attachment are rows of blond wood containers that refer without irony to Judd's sculpture. The counter consists of two thick glass blocks jutting out of a metal support, the whole effect achieved with meticulous craftsmanship. The lighting fixtures, simple metal parallelepipeds, stick out of the wall with no apparent effort. The few accessories—a ladder, a coat rack, a mirror—are presented with the same technical precision. The background light comes from a rectangle of opalescent glass, framed by a plain dark line, in which we can make out the blurry outline of fluorescent tubes.

The golden torso of a mannequin jutting out of the wall, a tall, narrow doorway, a mirror in the distance—Ocky's plays with an aesthetic that is spare and a little offbeat.

The shop front of plate glass rimmed by black brick, with the firm's logo imprinted on the window.

A neutral floor, pale walls and simple geometry make up the setting, in which each object is individualized. In the foreground, the counter formed by two thick slabs of glass suspended one over the other on a metal armature.

Opposite:
A black mannequin, cantilevered storage bins, a ladder of galvanized steel—minimalist to the hilt.

Details of the hanging
mechanism for
the glass tables and
counter. The precision
of execution is a crucial
element in the decor.

Plan and longitudinal
cross-section
of the premises.

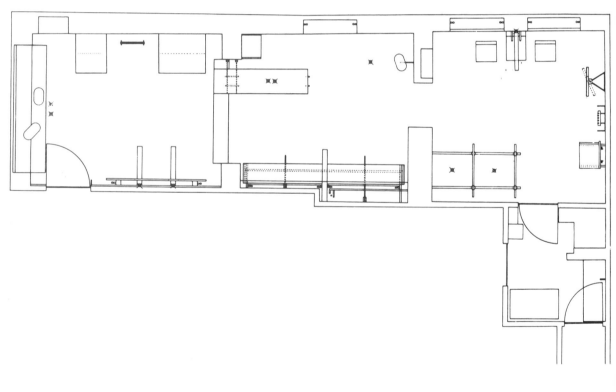

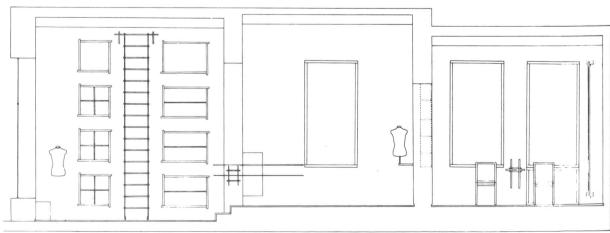

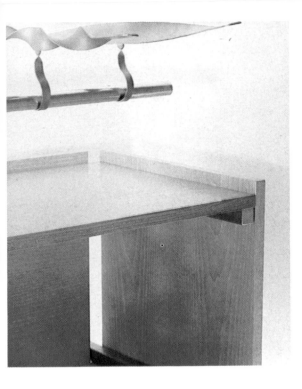

Detail of the "invisible"
hanging system
for the storage bins.

Detail of galvanized
steel clothes hanger.

The cantilevered counter.
In the background, the
opalescent glass lit from
behind by a sculpture
of fluorescent tubes,
an allusion to the work
of Dan Flavin.

The architect plays
on the the scarcity of the
materials—blond wood,
galvanized steel and thick
glass stand out against
a neutral background.

Try-on space: clothes
hanger and pivoting
mirror.

Shoebaloo Shoeshop
Amsterdam, The Netherlands

The walls of bright yellow and ocher red have been conceived as huge display cases for the products. With a multitude of little projecting platforms, they provide a display structure that is permanent yet extremely malleable: removable glass trays laid across two projections can hold one or several models at the same time.

Opposite:
At the rear of the shop, the try-on section with its soft carpeting is a blend of comfort and casualness. A multicolored and highly imaginative chair, which has, curiously, one too many legs (an amused reference to the specialty of the store?) waits for a customer. For the sales assistants, there are little padded stools covered in emerald green velvet.

All major port cities are cosmopolitan by their very nature. Sailors pass through, merchants establish trading posts and eventually come to stay. Nomads and tourists add a touch of the exotic. With its tracery of peaceful canals and twisting streets, Amsterdam is one of these open cities. It is not surprising that a Czech living in exile in neighboring Germany should be invited to exercise his talents here. All the more so as he is far from unknown. He arrived in the West at a time when design was breaking out of its functionalist corset to abandon itself to the riotous forms and colors offered by the Italians of the Memphis group. To the "new international style" expounded by Sottsass and his disciples, Boris Sipek could add his own native baroque note. For this shop situated in a quarter dominated by Dutch rationalism, his touch of Mitteleuropa was just the thing. The facade of Shoebaloo is immediately set apart from the building that houses it by its symmetry, its two curved windows and its color, an unusual ocher shade.

Shoebaloo Shoeshop is the name of a wholesale shoe company. On the walls on either side of the window, ornately curved metal rods hold high-heeled pumps and comfortable walkers for passers-by to see. Boris Sipek has renewed the

The floor covering
consists of broken terra
cotta tile surrounded
by white pebbles.
At the base of the wall,
a tile border of black and
white checks.

genre through a playful treatment of supports and color, but without affecting the functioning as a sales outlet whose needs are simple and straightforward. The long narrow premises break down quite naturally into display areas and try-on space. The wares are displayed against the walls on protruding blocks that support one, two or several shoes at a time, on a background of pure bright yellow. In the back, where shoes are tried on, an off-beat chair, a Freudian-looking couch and little stools with bright velvet cushions stand out against a wall with narrow slits that let light in from outside. As the small size of the store permits no stock or storage space, Boris Sipek has added some low black buffets that serve both as containers and display units, and topped them with amoeba-shaped glass plates. The floor is of red-ocher broken tile on a white pebble ground, a baroque look more Catalan than Prague. The yellow and ocher surfaces are set off at floor level by a black and white checkered border and at the top by a frieze of colored hearts. The lighting is a network of ceiling spots whose rays mingle with the light from the wall slits in the rear. In the central part of the shop, a series of light fixtures that look like medieval battle-axes lean nonchalantly against the walls, as if placed there at random. Shoebaloo Shoeshop combines a scrupulous design and careful attention to color and detail, with a relaxed and informal atmosphere so suitable to today's generation of shoppers.

Detail of the wall shelves used by themselves or with glass plates.

The central part of the store contains a number of small black chests with four chrome colonnettes holding a glass top of irregular shape. These double as storage containers to hold at least a small amount of stock.

Floor plan of the premises.

78 Shoebaloo Shoeshop, Amsterdam, The Netherlands

Opposite:

The facade, built outward from the door, creates a narrow doorway that slows down entry into the shop. The effect is to prolong a moment of suspense and heighten the curiosity aroused by the two curved windows of ocher red and gold.

Views from inside showing the shoe supports, curving metal rods sheathed in coral plastic. Their sinuous lines suggests some vegetal growth.

In the try-on area, a sofa as extravagant in its way as the five-legged chair. The indispensable mirror in which to admire one's newly-shod feet completes the decor. It leans against the wall, with a double frame that suggests a pair of wings about to take flight. The reflection shows the narrow openings in the rear wall that let in natural light.

Another view of the display area
with the little demonstration
counters.

Opposite:
The lighting of the central area
comes in part from these
implements (resembling some
medieval weapon!) that stand
casually leaning on the wall.

Details of wall brackets,
which occasionally hold decorative
objects; details of furniture
in try-on space.

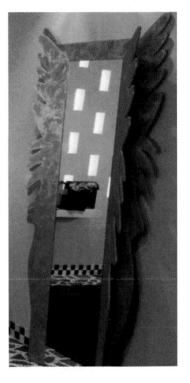

Jean-Louis Véret

Shu Uemura

Paris, France

Exterior night, exterior
day: two aspects of the
facade with its crowning
rotunda.
Details of little jars holding
the multicolored range
of make-up brushes.

Opposite:
In the front room, view
of the window. In the
foreground, a corner of
the glass-topped counter
on which a multitude
of accessories are set out
in jars or metal baskets.
As the endless variety
of implements would
suggest, beauty here
is taken as an art.

In the heart of Saint-Germain-des-Prés, the favorite quarter of artists and creators, stands the Paris shop of the Japanese cosmetic firm Shu Uemura International.

Clearly, its avant-garde design is quite in the spirit of the man who inspired it, the great Japanese make-up artist, Shu Uemura. As for integrating the space in the quarter, how else than through decoration and design, always subject to trends that are ever more ephemeral.

The impact of the facade on passers-by is instantaneous—particularly if the passer-by happens to be a woman. A cylindrical structure of wood and glass containing several display windows and surmounted by a brilliantly-lit sign on a circular panel. A second sign, this one vertical, stands in the doorway. The art of beauty underscores the distinct character of this place, a far cry from the traditional Paris *parfumerie*. The shop has a sales function, of course, but it is also a beauty salon where customers can receive advice on the art of being beautiful.

The plan of the shop clearly shows two well-differentiated spaces linked by a corridor. In the first room, make-up objects are displayed on a rectangular, glass table separated from the shop window by a low platform. Extending from this platform

The area that links the two main rooms takes into account
all the complexities of the shopper's feelings. On the left-hand side
all is glass and transparency under a cold light—an aseptic,
reassuring look. The polished granite floor and slim gray column
add calm and elegance. And for charm and comfort, the right-hand
wall is covered in blond wood.

is a granite counter backed against the wall and lit by an elongated mirror, an elegant way of limiting the area of the make-up salon. The white walls and granite slab flooring harmonize with the pale wood, creating an ideal setting to display and sample the beauty products.

Both in the window and inside the shop, the make-up objects are the predominant feature. Even more so on the shelves that completely fill the left side of the shop. The right side features a presentation table of blond wood and irregular structure, flush against the wall and rhythmically broken into different volumes.

Passing through the corridor, the visitor enters the second room, whose ceiling has a metallic structure supporting lamps and spotlights in an atmosphere resembling a movie set. A wooden counter in the shape of an irregular ellipse presents the lines of products on metal trays.

The Shu Uemura boutique, a typical space conceived along criteria of functionality and harmony, where all the elements work together toward a dual goal, the sale of products combined with an ensemble of beauty counselling. It is imbued with the spirit of well-balanced interiority and conceptual aesthetics traditionally present in the Japanese style.

Detail of a presentation table against the wall in the corridor.

Floor plan of the shop.

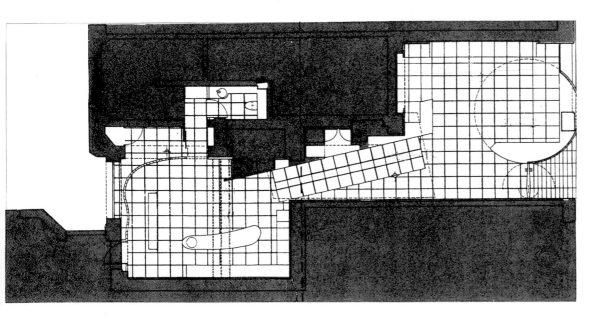

In the rear of the shop, the atmosphere
is halfway between laboratory
and movie set, between science and
artifice. On the ceiling is a range of lights
and projectors, while below, metal trays,
laid out with scientific precision
on the elliptical counter, show the various
product lines available.

Opposite:
Window display: a range of products
poured out into a variety of little bowls
and plates. Playing with the lure of color
and texture, the presentation suggests
fine craftsmanship or alchemy akin
to magic.

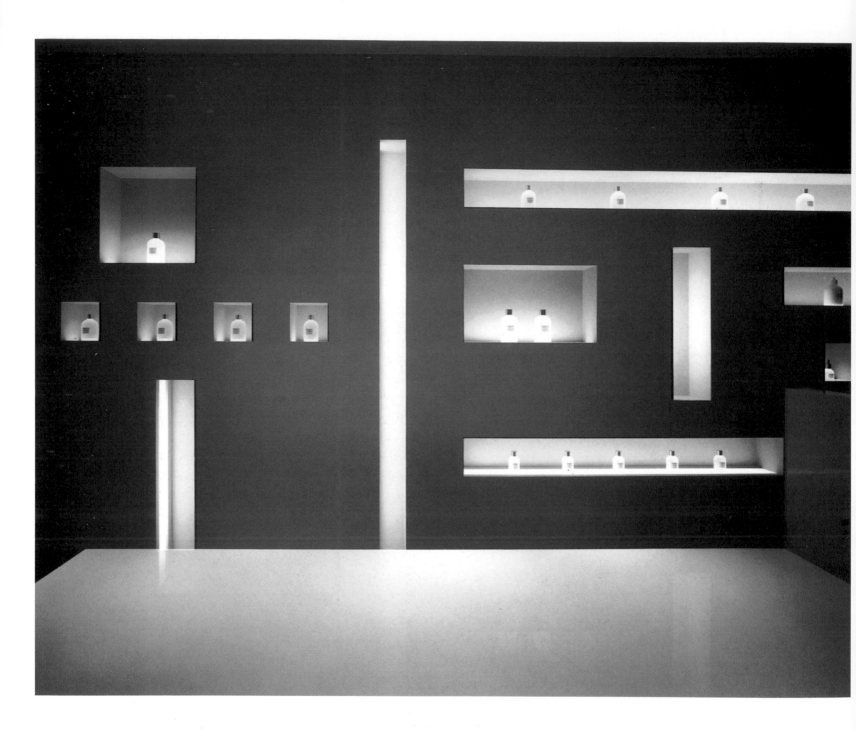

In both Dr. Baeltz shops, the decor consists
of showcases cut into the thick walls. Lit from
within, they create a striking geometry of light.
It is used to particularly stunning effect
in the smaller shop, a luminous assemblage
of verticals, horizontals and squares that evokes
some undecipherable cryptography.

Shigeru Uchida

Dr. Baeltz

Tokyo, Japan

The two shops created by Shigeru Uchida for Dr. Baeltz offer a perfect example of legibility between the nature of a product and the place destined for its sale. Small in size, they both integrate the ensemble of elements proposed in the range of Dr. Baeltz cosmetics into a single design that exhibits total symbiosis between aesthetic preoccupations and functional exigencies. The defining character of the Dr. Baeltz brand lies in the natural properties of the products. Extreme purity of lines, colors and volumes are therefore the outstanding feature in the design for their place of exhibition and demonstration.

In these premises the client is personally received by an esthéticienne (a beauty counsellor), whose role it is to advise each customer on the choice of products the best suited for her. The fact that this advisory function takes place up front, directly on street level, underscores the concern for direct, even intimate, communication that goes beyond the mere buying and selling relationship.

The impression given by both these spaces corresponds completely with what one may expect from the Dr. Baeltz line. No effort is made to attract the client's attention to the color or texture of the products offered, but simply to project an intuitive feeling that the entire Dr. Baeltz philosophy is aimed at waging an effective fight against the effects of wear and aging. The shop design is based on this implicit concept and the individual components are therefore totally minimized.

The all-glass facades deliver an immediate message, totally in phase with the company ethic. Here in the smaller shop the front is like a transparent jewel box that holds some rare and precious gem.

The transparency of the approach projects an idea of purity and a quest for perfection that is also expressed inside—in perfect accord with the brand image.

90 Dr. Baeltz, Tokyo, Japan

Opposite:

An identical feel pervades both
shops. In the larger one, we find
again the crystalline facade,
the elongated space bare but
for the table and two chairs and
the partition in the rear that
screens off the treatment area.
The same organization of
the display space, with cubbyholes
on the right and showcases
on the left, but this time there
is a single long narrow showcase.

Detail of the showcase showing
the treatment of the wall
with a covering of finely undulated
sand-colored wood.

The pleasing arrangement of cubbyholes and showcases functions as an element of lighting and decoration. Their functional use remains allusive. Products are sparsely placed, in small quantities, with some spaces left entirely empty, a discretion that underscores the rarity and value of the products.

In each space, the area has been structured in three parts: the boutique proper, a demonstration area and a zone for facial treatment located at the rear. The demonstration area is longitudinal and pared down to a strict minimum: a table and two steel-framed chairs covered with blue canvas. This is the only furniture in the shop. All the products are disposed around the periphery, directly integrated into the walls. A low partition separates the facial treatment zone from the rest of the shop. The fact that this partition does not reach the ceiling assures both physical and visual unity and guarantees the necessary continuity between the three component volumes.

All the originality of the interior design in fact rests on the way the products are presented. Packaged in simple transparent bottles, they are displayed in an orderly way in showcases cleverly cut into the long walls. At the same time, through their repetition and layout respective to one another, these hollows become an element of decoration. In the larger shop (38 m²), one long narrow showcase runs the entire length of the left-hand wall while the right-hand wall is filled from top to bottom with a series of square cubbyholes. In the other shop, we find the same cubbyholes opposite a varied pattern of showcases, creating an abstract composition of enigmatic charm. In both cases, the cleverly arranged lighting of each showcase adds to the plenitude of the space. The products appear as if on a stage. The small number of bottles on display projects a double message of scarcity and quality well in line with the spirit of the brand. This peripheral lighting is echoed by wells of light recessed in the ceiling, a combination producing a light that is uniform but never blinding.

The use of beige for all the walls and the elements of wood or resin combine to afford a sensation of great gentleness. Finely undulated wood, polished marble floor and a shop window entirely of glass—such details are the finishing touches in the overall design. Visual unity is total. The place is smooth, clear and transparent—like a complexion endowed with eternal youth.

The luminous horizon
of the wall showcase
and a resin demonstration
counter on two levels
separated by a vertical
structure.

Lluis Pau, Josep Martorell, Oriol Bohigas and David Mackay
Addicional
Olot and Banyoles, Spain

At the shop in Olot, passing from one level to another is an exercise in dynamics. The whiplash movement of the handrail, the dramatically-sloping inner wall, the wing-shaped counter supported by a sort of hunting trophy and even the famous bicycle chair by Achille Castiglioni.

The facades of the Addicional shops are an invitation to a show. The traditional shop window is replaced by this glass screen cut out of the wall and where the giant logo of the firm is superimposed on the vision of the interior arrangements.

Detail of standing lamps on display, which also add their light to the scene. They call to mind a lance thrust into molten gold.

Under the banner of Addicional, a chain of boutiques is developing in Catalonia, specialized in the sale of furniture, objects, lighting and accessories for the home. As the name implies, Addicional has excluded coordinated sets to give preference to single pieces and cult objects ranging from Mies van der Rohe's Barcelona chair to Aldo Rossi's coffee-pot. The task of inventing a setting that would be extremely flexible yet strongly identifiable for the design of its various boutiques was given to the most solid agency in Barcelona, whose international reputation is firmly established.

For the facades, the architects opted for a radical solution—to eliminate the traditional shop window altogether. The structure of the building is completely bared and in front of it is set a vast pane of glass in a metal frame or, as a variant, a luminous frame.

A red line on the upper part of the glass and the name Addicional below, written in letters 1,20 m high dispel all doubts as to the identity of the site.

Their second decision is one that permits all variations in all configurations: the original walls are bared to expose their surface, whether smooth or rough, with no wall covering and no false ceilings, then adorned with various intentionally strident colors. Perhaps paradoxically, the overall effect is to unite the spaces. The flooring is eclectic in nature, polished marble here, *chiné* carpeting there, elsewhere a floor made of slabs of glass. Furniture and objects are displayed in studied disorder on raised platforms of slatted wood. Lighting is dispensed from tracks that cast an indirect light, with some exposed light fixtures to complete the picture.

Another factor of identification: the handrail of the staircases is a simple black line of wrought iron with a whiplash curve, an allusion to Catalan *Modernismo*.

The architects have not only come up with a single sign to constitute the entire brand image, they have invented for the design of the Addicional shops a vocabulary and a syntax, not just a password but an entire statement to be recognized.

From the glass-paved
mezzanine, the first floor
stretches out like a vast
red-carpeted alley to
the far wall, hung with a
drapery of the same color.
The energetic colors give
a vigor to the ensemble,
which is accentuated
by the strong line
of the lighting track
that seems to cut right
through the vaults.

At night the view of the
Olot window is particularly
spectacular. An ample
curtain opens to reveal
a facade like a theater set,
a device undoubtedly
meant tongue in cheek,
judging from the white-
gloved hand on a metal
arm that holds the fold of
the curtain on the right.

View from the mezzanine
at the Banyoles store, in
which we can recognize
the decorative vocabulary
common to all the
branches of the chain. The
specific form of the
banister, the glass flooring
lit from below, the slatted
platforms. Distinctive here
is the oddly-shaped fresco
partially erased by the
yellow paint of the
roughcast wall.

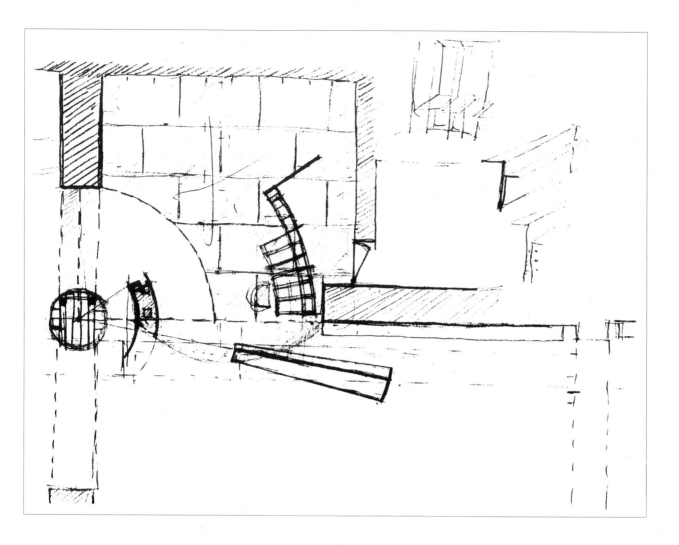

Architects' sketch of floor
plan.

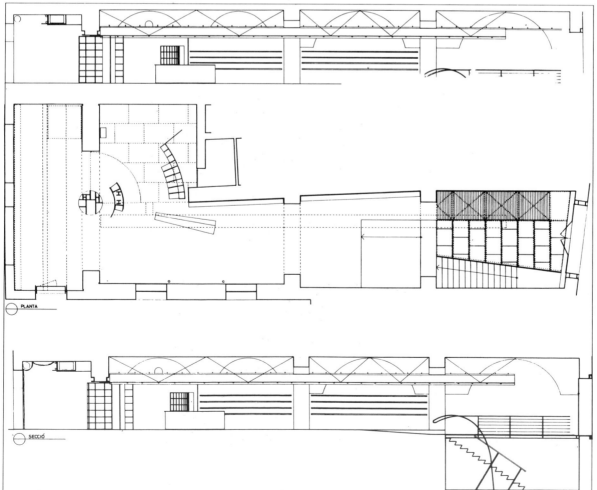

Plan and cross-section of
the Banyoles store.

Opposite:
Two views of the counter
area at Olot. The visitor
sees only the table,
a graceful wing of
engraved metal.
But under the staircase,
hidden from view, is a
small administrative space.

PLANTA

SECCIÓ

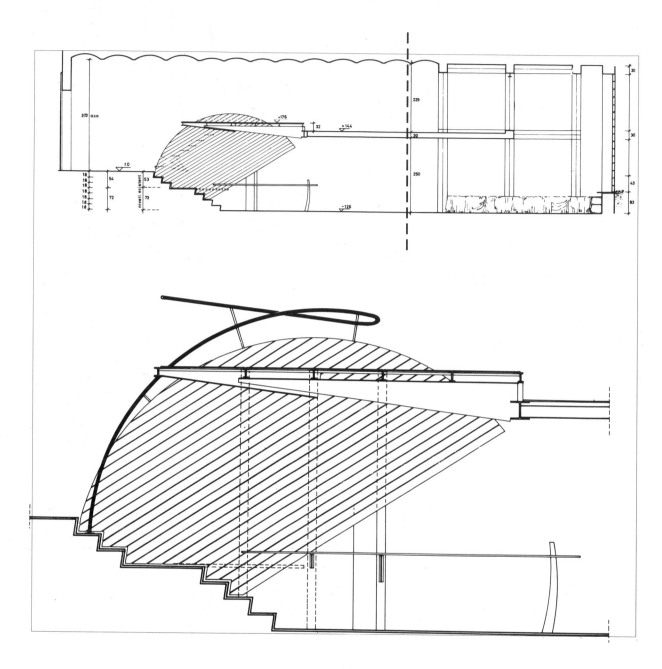

General cross-section
and detail of the passage
between the ground
and first levels, as it is
organized at Olot.

Opposite:
Different views
of the handrails. Above,
the mezzanine of the Olot
shop; below, the staircase
at Banyoles.

View of the first floor
exhibition space,
lit by a vast panel of natural
light. Here too a decisive
role is played by the acid
colors, whose boldness
and diversity contribute
to the image of the chain.

Opposite:
Geometry and pastel tones:
details of a staircase leading
to the ground floor.

Perry King and Santiago Miranda

Marcatré

Paris, France

It is no accident that office furniture is sold not in a store or a shop but in a place appropriately labeled showroom. Office furniture is chosen at least as much for its functional and ergonomic qualities as for its elegance or aesthetic appeal. A mass-produced and largely standardized product, it generally claims flexibility as its leading virtue, in the aim of giving company executives the feeling that, even with furniture that is relatively standard in design, they will be able to assert their own image and the culture of their firm. Whence the modern furniture showrooms, devoted not so much to simulating a true workspace as to suggesting the freedom with which the products can be used.

In 1989, when the company Marcatré, one of the greatest innovators in the field of office furniture, decided to open a branch in Paris, they quite naturally turned to their usual designers, Perry King and Santiago Miranda. Their studio, King and Miranda Associati, created in Milan in 1976, takes an interest in every facet of design—interior, industrial and graphic—and their creative approach seeks a dialogue between imagination and technique.

The problem before them was the following: to create a commercial space, defined as a showroom, distanced from the conventions proper to a shop. To begin with, the available premises presented structural drawbacks, but in the end they were used to good advantage to come up with an authentic exhibition area. The site was on the ground floor of a fairly recent building on Avenue Hoche and consisted of a series of shops and galleries laid out on a diagonal starting from a narrow facade.

The finished showroom reflects the spirit of seriousness and innovation that the company likes to offer its clients, a criterion that the Italian design team took into account. They added a pleasant and inviting work atmosphere, as the same space also contains the company offices. Disparities in the volumes and ceiling heights risked causing a loss of unity of space. As the budget did not permit them to remodel the interior structure, the designers opted for organizing the different areas independently of one another, which in no way hurts the harmony as a whole.

Three criteria guided this elegant realization. First, to transform the original rooms, giving them space and fluidity. Second, to create visual perspectives without architectural obstacles that could impede freedom of movement and the pleasure of contemplation. Lastly, to make the premises sufficiently attractive for the customers to want to enter in the first place. To this end, the authors created sectors

Getting the best of a structural defect: the awkward post in the middle of the facade has been hidden by a metal semi-circle that gives it a sculptural value. This central structure, nobly transformed, now focuses the entire window display.

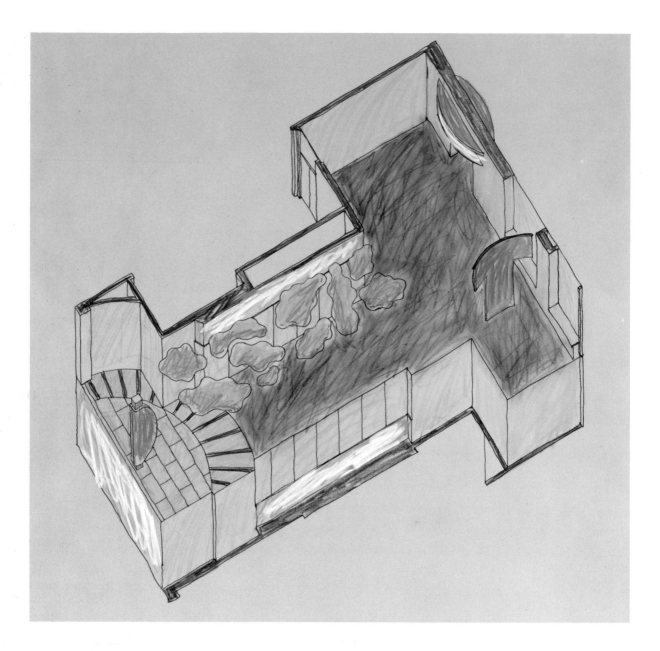

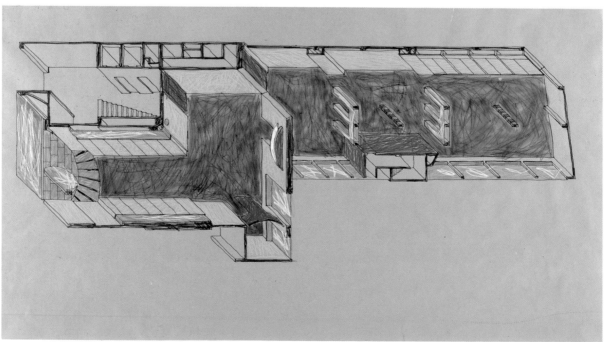

106 Marcatré, Paris, France

View of the hallway from
the rear of the showroom,
with the window display
visible in the distance.
The space stretches out
between two translucent
walls and under
an eternally blue sky
with myriad little lamps
suspended between
metallic gold clouds.

Another view of the hall
from the opposite
direction, from the shop
window toward the rear.

Opposite:
Axonometric drawings,
one showing the entrance
and display area, the
other, the entire space.

In the rear of the
showroom, a reception
area marked off from the
rest by a curved T-shaped
blue wall.

Opposite:
The translucent walls
of the central corridor
are adorned with a starlike
motif that resembles
frosted glass.

independent of one another, with volumes that suggested separation rather than actually creating it. Each area reflects a clearly-marked artistic conception. King and Miranda were able to harmoniously modulate the conceptual gap between the showroom as an exhibition site (with a commercial function but without sales) and the specifications proper to a shop.

The original premises had a glass facade that could easily have served as the main entrance. They chose to close off this entrance and to give access instead through the hall of the building. However, the transparent front was respected, enabling the eye to encompass a large display area. Starting with the various functional volumes available, they made the choice to install the main display areas in those that were on the avenue. The rear part contains the entrance from the hall of the building as well as the company offices.

Once the questions of circulation and apportioning of space were resolved, and the constraints of the site overcome, the architects went about making the entrance area and show window objects of attraction and spectacle. They marked the office entrance with tall twin porticoes, one simply painted in blue and white, the other its shadow, playing on the same colors by means of glass-enveloped tubes that shine with an intriguing glow. The show window was transformed into a little stage with, in the foreground, a pattern of veined gray marble with black marble highlights. The awkward central pillar is effaced by covering it with a heavy metal semi-circle, engraved with abstract signs that evoke some primitive rite. The long corridor that links the window to the back room is bordered by two translucent walls with crystal motifs reminiscent of frosted glass. Crowning the ensemble is a ceiling of midnight blue where clouds of gilded metal gleam in a pointillistic lighting.

Given a delicate question of interior design, King and Miranda answered with an intelligent and noble idea, giving Marcatré an exhibition space that is simple and at the same time strongly identified and which, beyond the quality of the products, suggests to the prospective user the freedom that the firm's furniture will afford him.

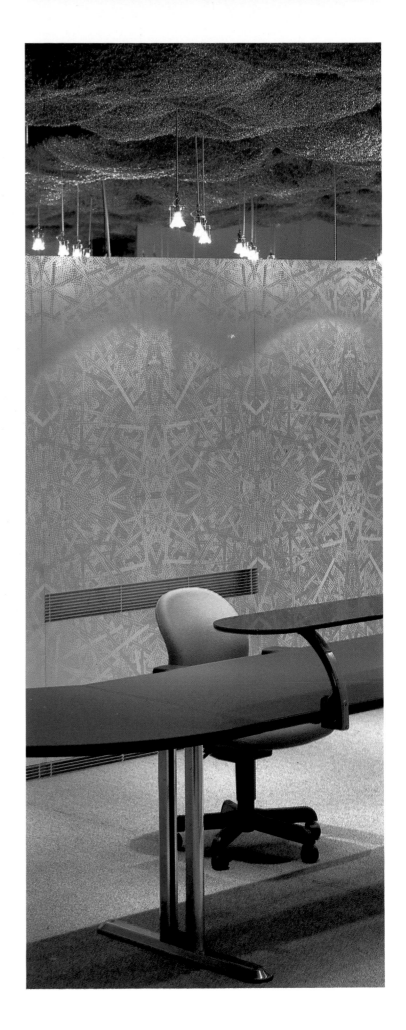

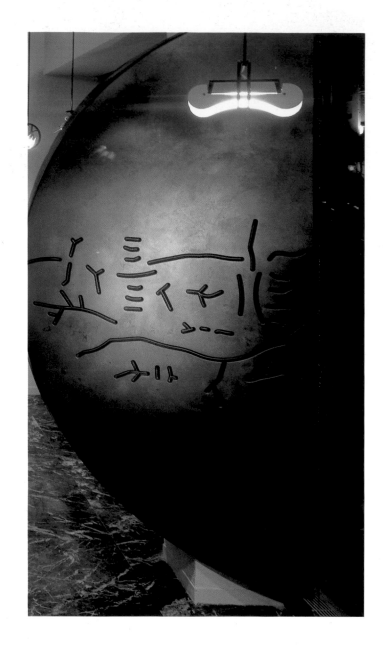

Detail of the metal
semi-circle in the window.
The carved signs appear
like some mysterious
primitive writing.

Opposite:
Display window seen
from the side. The circular
form of the marble floor
extends up to the corridor.

The passage from the showroom
proper to the office area is marked
by an entrance area surmounted
by a large glass ellipse,
a restatement in glass of the idea
of the blue sky covered
with clouds.

Opposite:
The office entrance is adorned
by a double portico made up
of striped blue and white pillars
in a casing of opalescent glass.
The light it casts is cool and
refreshing and the overall effect
is spectacular.

Cassina

Tokyo, Japan

Seen from the outside, the structure that has been inserted into the existing building appears through the glass facade. Color is of prime importance in this co-existence—Mario Bellini's warm red ocher, so typically Mediterranean, is courteously appended to the very mineral blue-gray of Japanese architect Tadao Ando.

In 1957 when Cassina launched the "superleggera" chair by architect Gio Ponti, it made the name of the firm as a producer of furniture that combined industrial know-how with the quality of artisanal production. It also confirmed their image as enlightened employers capable of choosing their designers from among the most talented young architects of the day. Among the "house" designers were Vico Magistretti, Afro and Tobia Scarpa and already the young Mario Bellini. By the 1970s there would also be the representatives of "radical" design, Gaetano Pesce and Archizoom. At the same time, Cassina made an international reputation by reproducing the sanctified heroes of the century: Frank Lloyd Wright, Mackintosh, Rietveld and Le Corbusier. The way was open to set up exhibition sites in all the capitals of the world.

The Tokyo showroom was a natural next step. Its opening may even seem a little late. But then, the Japanese are globe-trotters of insatiable curiosity.

The occasion presented itself at the beginning of the 1990s. There was a building in central Tokyo that already housed Italian firms: Krizia, Very Uomo, Gianni Versace. Moreover, the building was the work of one of the most famous and talented of Japanese architects, Tadao Ando.

Cross-section of the lower gallery.

Plans of the two levels.

Opposite:
Outer facade seen from another perspective.

View of one of the display areas where false windows in the pre-existing concrete wall are used as niches.

Behind the glass wall, the play of light on the upper gallery, where it narrows into a gangway.

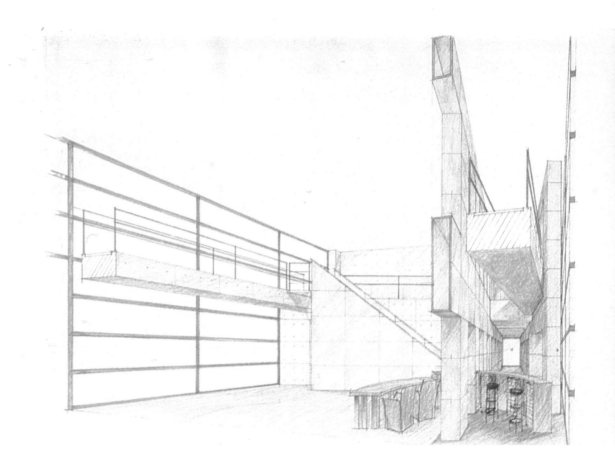

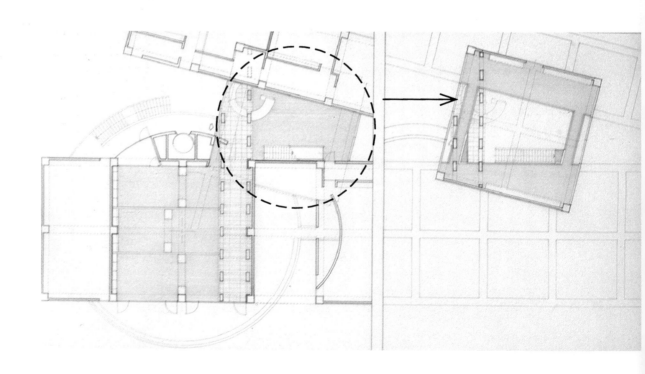

It took a certain temerity to affront the fine concrete lines of the master, not to mention tact and a bit of subtlety. Cassina called in a man who had worked with them over a long, faithful and fruitful career: Mario Bellini.

Bellini tackled the problem in a most civil manner. He built within the building of his his fellow architect in such a way as to be present but as light as possible, literally without touching the structure, except to skim the surface here and there. Into the existing geometry he inserted high walls of red sienna colored stucco (a color whose secret only the Italians possess) pierced with two rows of classic empty windows, in the manner of an urban landscape by De Chirico. The lower space remains empty while in the upper part the circulations between the two structures, between stucco and concrete, are on uniform wood floors. The only foreign (therefore exotic) object is a sculptural but minimal staircase covered with riveted panels of galvanized sheet metal. A series of spots complete the design, projecting theatrical shadows on the metaphysical decor. The notion of exhibition is hardly present—the furniture is scattered helter-skelter through the galleries, as if left there at random to punctuate the visitor's path. Here a Mackintosh chair, there a table by the trio Le Corbusier-Perriand-Jeanneret, elsewhere a leather chair by Bellini himself.

The Italian architect has fulfilled Cassina's expectations by cautiously inserting himself within his Japanese host, a fitting Western response to the exquisite politeness of the Land of the Rising Sun.

View from the top of the stairs,
showing the position of the windows
in the upper gallery and the lower level.

Opposite:
Placing the galleries around the periphery
liberates a large, totally empty space on the
first level. In the foreground, the staircase,
a double triangle of galvanized metal,
is a striking sculptural creation. The riveted
plates that cover its sides are similar in form
and color to the geometric treatment
of the concrete walls all around.

On the ground floor, we
see the entrance to the
showroom. The pieces
on display are dispersed
over the parquet floor as
if at random.

Opposite:
A building within
a building, or better yet,
a sort of Mediterranean
city recreated in the heart
of a Japanese edifice.
There is something
moving in this osmosis,
accomplished as it is with
respect for the creative
and cultural identities of
both parties. This inspiring
quality is accentuated
by the celestial creatures
flying on the ceiling.

In a courtyard in the
Chalk Farm district,
a small brick building
painted blue. Arad has
preserved some signs
of aging: the steep
stairway, rusty gratings
of expanded metal,
and even a prop that
resembles scaffolding.
On the roof, three
stainless steel chairs
made in the workshop.

Ron Arad
One Off
London, England

The One Off studio founded by Ron Arad has led a nomadic existence. After Covent Garden, where it first made its name, and Shelton Street, which marked Arad's earliest work with soldered metal, it has now moved to Chalk Farm, the district favored by trendy London. In a poorly paved courtyard once occupied by old craft workshops, One Off has set up shop in a small shabby building, whose old brick walls have been brightened up with a thick coat of electric blue paint. The ground floor soldering shop where Arad once produced, with his own hands, the twisted metal furniture that made him famous, has now become a quieter spot where One Off produces models and complex computer programs. A stairway like that on a freighter and a long gangway of slightly rusty expanded metal lead to the upper level. In a long narrow quadrangle some 50 meters by 12, Arad has put together his architecture and design bureau with his furniture display showroom, all under one roof. And what a roof it is! A curved metal structure supports a mesh of expanded metal, itself covered by translucent PVC. No screen or wall separates the showroom from the architect's office: the more subtle boundary is between the rippling wooden floor of the showroom that seems to be lifted up by a huge wave and the quiet planes of the workspace. A large metal arch that looks as if it holds the air conditioning shaft joins the crest of the wave to a mezzanine where the master meditates some startling new idea. The den, surprising for a visitor, is the designer's natural workspace as well as a manifesto of his art.

Arad occupies a most particular place in the world of architecture and design. The only tradition he seems to evoke is that of expressionism: he agrees that he feels more influenced by Frederick Kiesler—the only architect close to surrealism—than by the straight-lined reasonableness of the moderns. A student, though hardly a disciple, of the Architectural Association of London, a designer who scorns method, an artisan dubious about the value of technical prowess, Arad has traced his own road, following his curiosities and interests of the moment. Today others produce the furniture and objects whose sensual resources he has finished exploring. For his new projects, he has gone over to more complex techniques, where computer technology has a new role to play. He resorts to scientific programs like the Dassault firm's Katya, which enables the user to design the object while simultaneously creating the tool for its production. But Arad has not given up working in public: the showroom is at the same time a state of his art and a pretext to exchange ideas with his visitors, his way of remaining in touch with the world.

Night-time view:
the metal structure
supporting the roof
calls to mind
calligraphic signs.

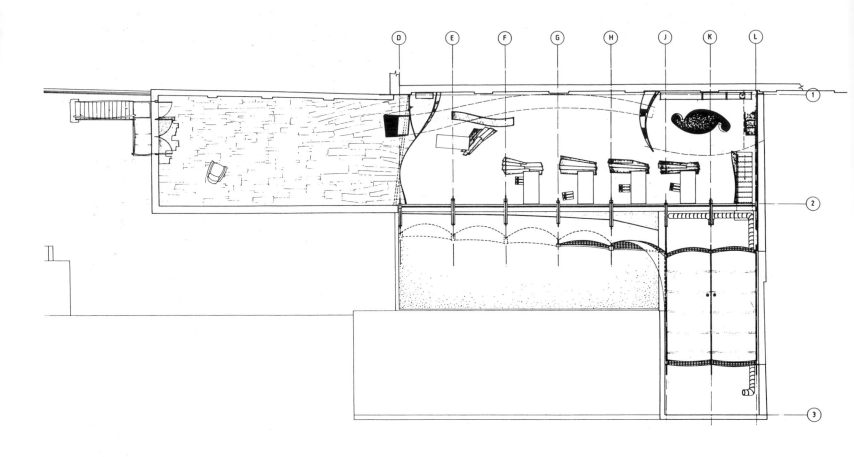

Cross-section of
showroom and
workshop. The arch,
which runs from
the floor wave to
the mezzanine, is both
a support for displaying
items and a utilities
shaft.

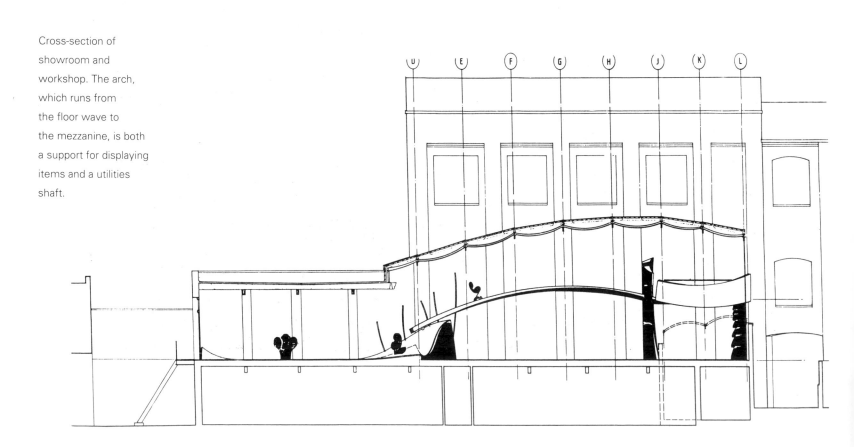

The showroom area
with the wave in the
floor.

The arch used
as a support for
displaying objects.

The architectural office,
showing the ribbed
ceiling, the metal netting
and the translucent PVC
covering.

Carlotta de Bevilacqua and Federica Galbusiera
Artemide
Los Angeles, United States

For its new California showroom, Artemide has chosen this simple warehouse. A large box-shaped structure, built on a single level, its appeal lay in its ample size and the authenticity of its building style, all brick and wood. Added to this was the historic attraction of the site, still steeped in memories of old Hollywood—it had served for a long time as a storehouse for movie costumes.

Opposite:
The basic idea of the two architects was to create a structure without altering the style. Despite the partitioning of the space—which was essential, as other brands and designers exhibit here as well—the visual communication is unimpeded. Wherever you stand you can appreciate the impressive volume of the warehouse with its immense wooden ceiling.

Artemide is part of a long beautiful tradition of Italian lighting design. Over the years the firm has called on a host of great designers from the Italian peninsula, from Enzo Mari to Achille Castiglioni, from Sottsass to Gismondi, from Mangiorotti to Richard Sapper. Through the years it has developed an ample range of a particular, identifiable culture, which accords equal importance to lighting and to light fixtures, and thus, a style of exhibiting their products that allows for some rather perilous juxtapositions.

For its new showrooms in Los Angeles, Artemide has taken its distance from the Design Center and Melrose Avenue where all the trendy design is concentrated, and picked a location in tune with the times. The fact that it chose Culver City, just in the early stages of rebirth under the impetus of developer Frederick Smith and architect Eric Moss, shows the new interest aroused by the quarter. The site is a brick warehouse, a simple box of the sort that Los Angeles small industry produced by the thousands, modest hangars with a plain wood structure and whose interior volumes combine space with reassuring proximity.

The architects Carlotta de Bevilacqua and Federica Galbusiera have managed to fit in well with local culture by coming up with a meticulous dosage of California mellow and Italian formalism: polished concrete floors, bare walls and ceilings, slatted partitions and simple wooden posts, in sharp

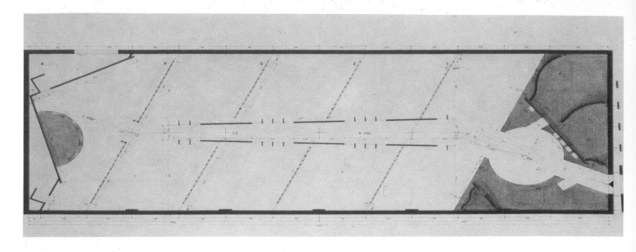

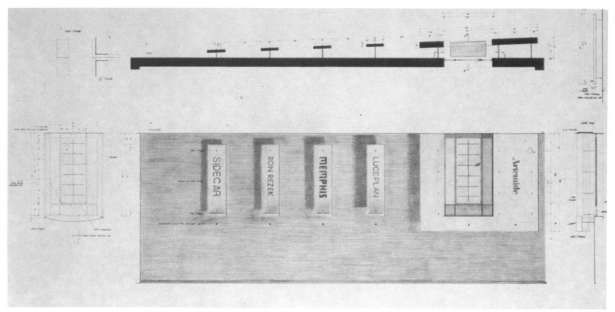

Plans of the premises:
at either end a vestibule
with a raised platform
for theatrical effect.
In the center, the space
for the various exhibitors
is divided diagonally
and linked by a narrow
circulation corridor.

contrast to which they use a theatrical manner of presentation, where disparate objects and lighting fixtures, set out on platforms, seem to be performing on stage.

Other collections aside from Artemide's are shown in this space, like those of Ron Rezek, one of California's best designers, or those of the firm Luce-Plan. For this reason, it was necessary to design a circulation and partitions in order to distinguish the products of one or another. The result is a free-spirited space, like a street lined with open areas, or a tidy, straight-lined souk. The approach resembles that of a museum, presenting refined objects in such a way that can only hasten their consecration.

At the end opposite
the entrance, a room built
around a deliberately
theatrical decor, a
semi-circular stage with
a huge white screen
for a backdrop.

View of the entrance
vestibule, where
they have once again
created a dramatic
atmosphere through
the use of platforms
and walls arranged like
in a theater set.

Opposite:
The area allocated
to each exhibitor is
bordered by huge wooden
frames from which items
can be hung but which in
no way impede the view.

The narrow central
corridor that leads to the
display areas accentuates
the great length of
the building. It has been
inserted like a tube down
the middle of the
showroom's open space.

Opposite:
The entrance vestibule
seen from another angle.

General view from the
entrance: the rounded
platforms compose a vast
circle, off-center in
relation to the main axis.

Achille Castiglioni
Flos
Milan, Italy

You follow the corridor
as you would a street,
walking between walls
treated like metallic stone
facades, from which
you discover the adjoining
display spaces—be it a
simple niche, a recessed
wall or a whole small
room. What is essential
is the diversity of the
display. It must surprise
the visitor, offer multiple
perspectives, suggest
all kinds of cases that will
give him ideas for
decoration and new
lighting uses.

The showroom of the famous Italian lighting firm Flos has been established for many years now on the Corso Monforte in the center of Milan. It was remodeled several times, always by the hand of the master, Achille Castiglioni, with whom the firm has had close relations for a long time. It was for Flos that Castiglioni designed some of his masterpieces, in particular a certain lamp made of an auto headlight perched on a metal stalk, a sort of do-it-yourself dream construction, the ironic adaptation of an industrial object for domestic use.

Traditionally, the Flos showroom met certain well-defined criteria. It was intended to exhibit lighting rather than objects,

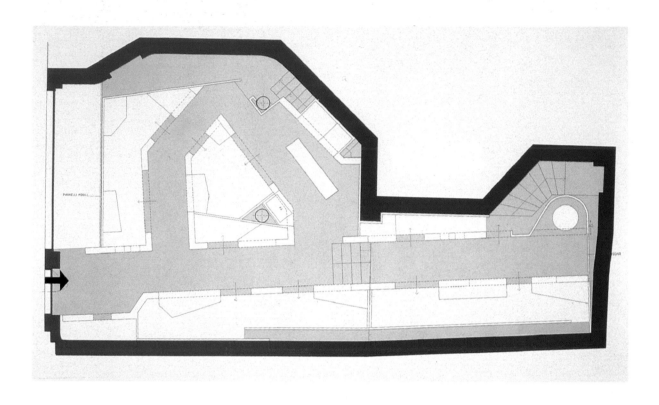

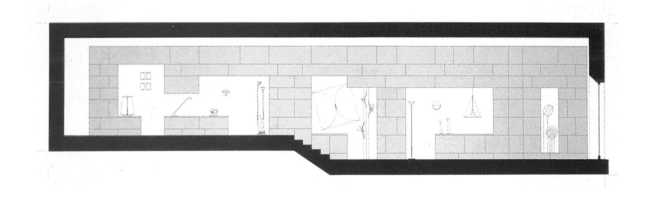

Floor plan and longitudinal cross-section
of the showroom.

Opposite:
View down the narrow corridor
with the glass door of the entrance
at the end. The dark-covered ceiling fades
into obscurity, giving an impression
of height that makes up for the narrow
width of the passage.

and therefore had a precise distribution that assigned each apparatus a specific space that would demonstrate its particular qualities, whether power, color or scope... With the ever-growing number of models, a new strategy had to be adopted. The various appliances are here displayed not by family responding to a particular function but grouped together like a vision of coexistence in a given space. For example: a suspension hangs next to a wall bracket or a floor lamp.

The premises are long but of medium size (110 m²) and Castiglioni opted for a functional approach that would also be elegant and playful. Through the longest length, he traced a sort of street, increasing the dimension even more by adding a mirror at the end. This street is lined with thick walls in metallic tones that bear a strange resemblance to the building stone of Milan. It gives the impression that every display space, each with an original configuration, constitutes a little show window offering itself to the visitor's gaze. The limestone floor has been left as it was originally. The ceiling is effaced by a dark covering. Here and there, discreet signs punctuate the metallic walls—coded numbers like those in a catalogue, or a repetition of the firm's logo. The light fixtures are presented with all the diversity demanded by the range of Flos products. A single object, another icon of radical Italian design, the Archizoom console, with its fine white ceramic grid, dialogues with the Arco, one of the most subtle lamps of the master Castiglioni.

The complexity of this space—with all its angles, recesses and protrusions—recalls the varied configurations of domestic space. The architectural artifice also evokes the many possible cases where furniture dialogues with lighting. The openings and niches further serve as tables and shelves, as the showroom has practically no furniture, except for the tiled Archizoom console on which is perched the graceful Arco lamp.

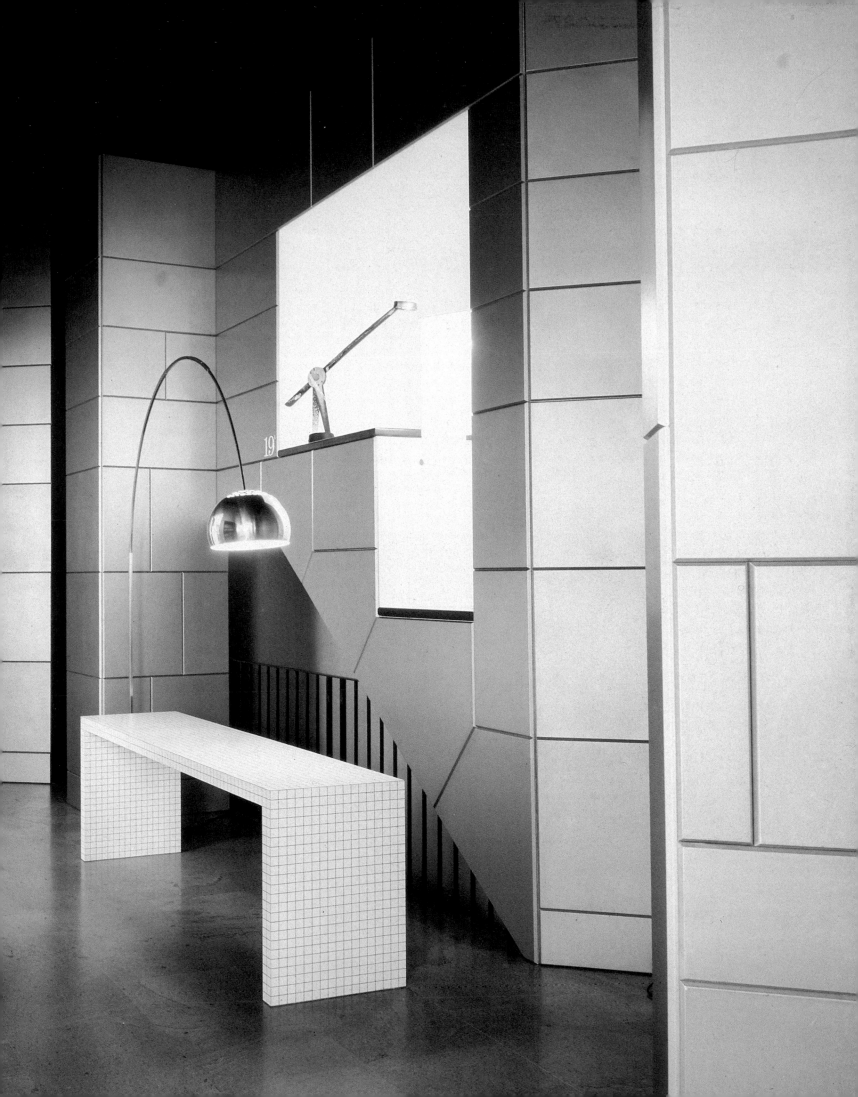

Another view
of the corridor.

Opposite:
The path of this narrow
passage-way is infinitely
multiplied by a large
mirror on the rear wall.

The smooth light walls
inside the niches and
recesses act as reflectors,
amplifying the light
diffused by the appliances.

They have their exits and their entrances; And one man in his time
plays many parts. At first the infant. Then the whining schoolboy with
shining morning
Unwilling to school. And
a woeful ballad Made to his mistress
quick in quarrel, Seeking the
And then the justice, Full of wise
shifts Into the lean and
again toward childish treble
Last scene
and mere
the past, present,
and future can be
experienced through
storytelling
searching the new

Fitzgerald, Roche, Cicio and Hambrecht

Tempus Expeditions

San Diego, United States

A 21st-century Ali Baba's
cave: an explosion
of colors, an infinity
of objects and, featured
in the window, two
cultural references,
an ancient statue and a
pseudo-medieval column.

Opposite:

A Greek ephebe seems
to have left his pedestal,
irresistibly drawn by
this display, and steps
through the plate glass
on which is printed a
quote from Shakespeare.
Could it be that art is best
selling point?

The lively competition that reigns in the retail trade stimulates the imagination of entrepreneurs and consequently that of designers. In the 1980s retail firms began to resort to all forms and techniques of spectacle that would dramatize or show off their merchandise. The more sensationalistic it grew, the more ephemeral became the trends. With the growth of electronics, generalized communication and techniques of simulation, a new concept of commerce, a new kind of sales outlet, has come into being. It too is a form of spectacle, but it has deliberately chosen to use software instead of hardware, thereby conferring total versatility on any realization. Now all you have to change is a computer chip when yesterday you had to re-do the decor of a shop. The products themselves follow a logic of theme rather than domain of use. The new sales spaces have taken over (and turned upside down) the idea of the theme parks, where selling is no longer a marginal activity, but a central one that conditions and renews the spectacle.

William K. Sadleir conceived the project Tempus Expeditions, starting from the observation that in America every year, there are more people who visit malls than who visit Disneyland.

His creation, implanted in San Diego's Mall of America, tries to be a synthesis between sales area and amusement park, with some educational aspects to boot. In a word, Tempus Expeditions covers a vast range: the name itself permits of every variation and permutation of travel, whether in time or space. A 42-seat movie theater, two movement simulation

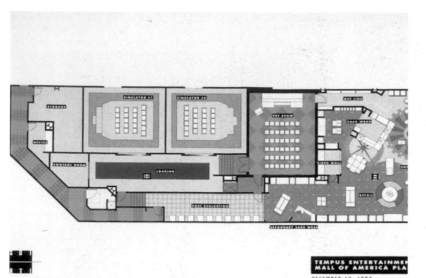

cabins of 21 seats each, batteries of interactive video monitors and an extensive use of audiovisual techniques alternate with more traditional selling space with their shelves, racks and display cases.

The task of designers FRCH was complex: following a program worked out by marketing experts and complicated by heavy technical constraints caused by the needs of electronics and spectacular display, the mission of FRCH included not only the design of the sales space but also the logo of the firm, its identifying marks and packaging.

The theme chosen, which embraces the ideas of progress and of man's ingenuity, offered a wide field for metaphor, and FRCH threw themselves wholeheartedly into the game. From the ancient athlete going through the glass barrier and running toward a Venus crowned by a dome simulating the celestial vault (thanks to electronics) to monitors posed on fluted columns, all manner of juxtaposition is permitted. The products have been chosen for their relation (close or distant) to the theme or with the imagery referring to it: a multitude of electronic gadgets rub shoulders with cult designer objects—vintage-looking toasters, diving helmets—as well as with T-shirts and aviator jackets. Tempus Expeditions presents itself as the post-modern sales space par excellence. The decor is eclectic and highly visual. It exploits the most popular clichés—classic statuary, Chaplin's *Modern Times* with the giant gears of the assembly line... Nor is it afraid to wink in the direction of great men, prominently quoting Shakespeare's soliloquy: "All the world's a stage..." Another quote from the Bard might also be appropriate: "We are such things as dreams are made of..."

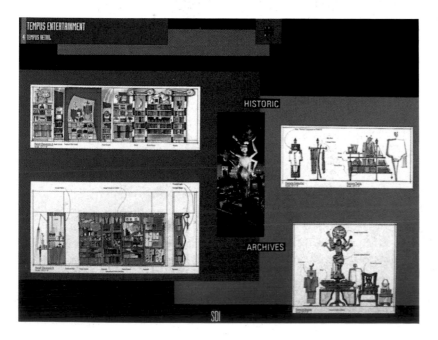

Ground plan and sketch showing an early version of the shop window. Studies showing the various display structures.

A corner of the sales area lit by opalescent blocks over the display cases and by ceiling spots. The carpeting repeats the pattern of letters and numbers.

Monitors perched
on fluted columns,
surmounted by strange
or baffling portraits.

In the entrance area,
the gigantic gears from
Chaplin's *Modern Times*,
a cultural cliché, are
suspended from
the ceiling and silhouetted
on the floor.

Two-colored columns
topped with Ionic capitals
decorate the racks where
a vast assortment
of heterogeneous objects
is displayed, like a
contemporary version
of an urban *souk*.

View of the area
containing the simulation
booths. An eerie setting
where a ceilingful of
saucer-like objects cast
their blue light into
the semi-darkness.

Opposite:
In this sales space,
the central focus is
a star-spangled cupola
where a Venus de
Milo stands, showing off
her mechanical arms.

Architects' biographies

ARAD, RON

Born in 1951 in Tel Aviv.
Studied at the Jerusalem Academy of Art (1971-1973), then at the Architectural Association of London (1974-1979).
Based in London since 1973.
In 1981, created the One Off workshop for the conception/design, production and distribution of furniture with Caroline Thorman at Covent Garden.
In 1989, founded Ron Arad Associates with Caroline Thorman at Chalk Farm Road (London), in which One Off was integrated in 1993.
In 1994, installed Ron Arad Studio in Como (Italy), a workshop for the production of limited series,
Visiting professor at Vienna Hochschule (1994-1997). Taught design at RCA in London.
Directed several design workshops for students: at the Vitra Design Museum in Weil am Rhein Germany, at the Vitra Farm in France and in Ravenna, Italy.
Named Designer of the year, in 1994.

Principal realizations:

Furniture and design: Well-Tempered Chair (1986) and Schizzo Chair (1994) for Vitra International, Switzerland; in Italy, Spring Collection (1990), Misfits chairs (1993) and Sof-Sof (1995) for Moroso, TV/video furniture for Hotel Zeus (1992) and furniture for the Anonymous cafés (1994), for Noto, Empty-Chair, conceived for the foyer of the Tel Aviv Opera the table Fly Ply (1993) produced by Driade, lighting system (1996) for Artemide, Fantastic Plastic Elastic chair (1996-1997) for Kartell, CD storage systems (1997) for Alessi; office accessories (1991) for Lippert Wilkins and sofa (1994) for Draenert, in Germany...

Architecture:
Bazaar boutique for Jean-Paul Gaultier.
In London (1984); One Off showrooms in Covent Garden (1983-1986); fashion boutiques Milano Monamour in Milan, Equation in Bristol, England, and Camomilla in Rome; publishing house in Schopfheim, in the Black Forest(1993); Michelle Mabelle boutique on Via della Spiga in Milan (1994); foyer of new Opera House, Tel-Aviv (1989-1994); office building "Y" in Seoul (1995); restaurant Belgo Centraal in London (1995); art gallery Achenbach in Düsseldorf (1995); Adidas Stadium complex in Paris (1995-1996); first "Sport Café" of a chain of cafés-restaurants for Adidas/Kronenbourg in Toulon (1997); private homes in London and Israel (1997); Domus Totem for magazine Domus in Milan (1997).

BELLINI, MARIO

Born in 1935 in Milan.
Graduated from Milan Polytechnic University (1959).
Founded his agency in 1962 in Milan.
In 1963, in charge of design at Olivetti where he created three winners of the SMAU prize, the calculator Divisumme 18, typewriter Praxis 35 and the portable Quaderno.
In 1972 participated in MOMA exhibition, Italy: The new domestic landscape, with his mobile environment Kar-a-Sutra.
Collaborated with auto companies Fiat and Lancia, then Renault, for whom he designed the Espace.
Bellini taught at the Institute of Industrial Design, University of Venice (1959-1962), at the Hochschule für Angewandte Kunst in Vienna (1982-1983) and at the Domus Academy of Milan (1983-1985).
Editor-in-chief of Domus (1986-1991).

Compasso d'oro 1962, 1964, 1970, 1986.
Twenty-five of his objects are in the permanent collection of MOMA, which held a monographic exhibition of his work in 1987.

Principal realizations:

Design: canapé Amanta (1966) for C&B and B&B, leather armchair and sofa (1967) and Cab chair for Cassina (1977), TV and radios for Brionvega, Hi-fi equipment and electric organs for Yamaha, lighting fixtures for Artemide and Flos, office furniture for Vitra...
Architecture: showroom Cassina in Milan (1968), Interdecor in Tokyo (1981), residential buildings, Brera district of Milan (1987), business center Yokohama Business Park in Tokyo (1987), Design Center, Gotanda Station, Tokyo (1987), Television Exchange Center in Shanghai (1988), office complex Via Kuliscioff in Milan (1982-1988).

BEVILACQUA (DE), CARLOTTA

Born in 1957.
Graduated from Polytechnic of Milan (1983). Worked at firm of her mother, Franca de Bevilacqua, then produced exhibition settings for the companies Esma, Artemide, Moda Movie Monde, as well as for the Triennale de Milan.

Realizations in Italy: building restructuration in conjunction with the residential and commercial project Montorio al Vomano (1985-1988), center for CISI/Telecommunications Show (1986); showroom Artemide, with Federica Galbusieri, in Los Angeles (1987-1988); houses Maschio-Broto and Mangiavacca Vimercate o Paladino, in Milan, Steinmann house in Portofino (1988-1990).

GALBUSIERI, FEDERICA

Born in 1961 in Pavia, Italy
From 1983 worked for Marco Dezzi Bardeschi, Mario Bellini, Claes Oldenburg, Frank O. Gehry; in 1990, with Massimo Ansbacher; in 1991, for Gregotti Associati International and the Milan office of Paolo Ferrari.

Realizations: partial restructuration of a farm in Galliavola, with Giulio de Carli (1985-1986), a country house in Stradella (1988-1989); an apartment P. Sarpi Street in Milan, with Serena Arribaldi (1989-1990).

CASTIGLIONI ACHILLE

Born in 1918 in Milan.
Brother of Piergiacomo (1913-1968) and Livio (1911-1979), architect-designers, both of whom he worked with at various times over the years (with Livio until 1952, with Piergiacomo until his death). The first firm of the three together saw the creation of a radio for Phonola and, in 1938, a silverware service named Caccia, for Alessi (re-edited in 1990).
Graduated from the U Politecnico of Milan (1944).
Taught at the school of architecture, then at the school of interior architecture at the Polytechnic of Turin, later at Milan.
In 1995, Le Printemps du Design paid tribute to the three Castiglioni brothers.

Principal realizations:

Design: with Piergiacomo, lamps Tubino for Flos (1951) and Luminator for Arform (1955, Compasso d'oro 1957), Spalter vacuum cleaner for Rem (1956), Mezzadro chair (1957) re-edited by Zanotta in 1971, children's camera (1958), lamp Taraxacum (1960) and light fixture Arco (1962) for Flos, Hifi RR 126 for Brionvega, table Cacciavite for Bernini (1966), prie-dieu chair Primate (1979) which is in the collection of MOMA, New York, and Kunstgewerbe in Zurich; after

the death of Piergiacomo: lamps Parentesi (with Pio Manzu), Frisby, Taraxacum for Flos, low tables Servo Muto (1974) and Cumano for Zanotta (1979-Compasso d'oro 1981), glassware Ovio and Pario for Danese, bed Ittiti for Interflex (1986)...

Architecture: high-rise office buildings Permanente in Milan (1952), parish church San Gabriele (1959-1960).

FONT, JOSEP

Born in Santa Perpetua de la Mogoda, Spain.
Studied stylism in Barcelona.
Associated with stylist Luz Diaz, with whom he created the brand "Mapamundi." In 1988 he started the knit collection "JFLD," sold in Spain, France, Italy, Belgium, London and Chicago.
Josep Font and Luz Diaz formed a company for the production and distribution of their brand and opened shops in Barcelona, then in Bilbao.
Has worked alone since 1995. In November 1997, presented his 1998 spring/summer collection in Tokyo.
Elected "Centimeter" of the year 1996, by the circle MODA FAD, in Barcelona.

Realizations: scenography of showrooms "—Josep Font y Luz Diaz" 106, Paseo de Gracia, in Barcelona (1991) and Iparraguirre, 38, in Bilbao (1992); furniture in collaboration with Oscar Tusquets (1997).

FRCH DESIGN WORLD WIDE

Created in 1968, the American agency FRCH (Fiztgerald, Roche, Cicio & Hambrecht) has developed an extensive consultantcy in architecture, design and company image, in the sectors of retail, leisure, hotels and financial markets. Using the services of some 200 specialists, architects, designers, graphic artists, marketing professionals... in its offices in New York, Cincinnati and Singapore, FRCH has won over such companies as Discovery Channel, Old Navy, Nike, etc.

Among its recent projects: in the United States, the shops of Harrah's Casino in Las Vegas, interior decoration of Eddie Bauer's in Chicago and the music department of Barnes & Noble in Livonia (Michigan), the logo and graphic identity of the bookshops Borders, design of an Oshkosh B'Gosh shop in Leawood (Kansas) and Tempus Expeditions in San Diego.

In charge of project Tempus Expeditions, San Diego:

McGOVAN, STEVEN P.

Graduated from the University of Ohio.
Began as a theater decorator for Kings Productions/Paramount Parks.
Also worked for Fox and Hanna-Barbera.
Vice-president of agency FRCH, director of design department.
Member of International Association of Amusement Parks and Attractions (IAAPA).
Member of the jury of the University of Cincinnati's College of Design, Art, Architecture and City Planning.

HORWITZ, THOMAS

Graduated from the University of Cincinnati.
Decorator for the company Winegardner & Hammons (hotel industry), for whom he created prototypes for the interior design of hotel chains Radisson, Holiday Inn and Homewood Suites.
Senior Vice-president of FRCH, managing principal-Cincinnati.

BEEGHLY, MICHAEL

Graduated from the Art Academy of Cincinnati.
Joined FRCH in 1985. Senior Vice-president.
Member of AIGA (American Institute of Graphic Arts), SEGD (Society for Environmental Graphic Design), International Council of Shopping Centers and IAAPA.

IDP - INTERIORS DISSENY

BOHIGAS, ORIOL

Born in 1925 in Barcelona.
Graduated from the Escola Tecnica Superior d'Arquitectura of Barcelona (ETSAB) in 1951.
Doctorate in 1963.
In 1951, partnership with Josep Martorell.
Professor at ETSAB (1964-1966), then director (1977-1980).
Planning advisor to the mayor (1984), then cultural advisor of the city of Barcelona (1991-1997).
Professor emeritus of the Polytechnic University of Barcelona (1995).
President of the Joan Miró Foundation (1981-1988).
Gold Medal for artistic merit of the city of Barcelona (1986) and innovation award Voker Stevin (1992).

MACKAY, DAVID

Born in 1933 in Eastbourne, Sussex, England.
Architecture degree from Northern Polytechnic of London (1958).
Settled in Barcelona in 1959.
Joined firm of Martorell and Bohigas in 1962.
Director of the Foreign Studies Program of the Catholic University of America in Barcelona (1981-1986).
Visiting professor at University of Washington in St. Louis (1981) and the architecture school of the University of Wisconsin in Milwaukee (1986).
Professor at ETSAB (1985-87).
Andrew N. Prentice Prize 1960 of the Royal Institute of British Architects, for his study of Spanish architecture.

MARTORELL, JOSEP

Born in 1925 in Barcelona.
Doctorate in architecture.
In 1951, partnership with Oriol Bohigas.
Since the 1950s, has been involved in various local groups responsible for planning and heritage preservation in Barcelona and more widely in Catalonia.
In 1985 co-authored the project to redesign the Barcelona seafront.
From 1987 to 1989, technical director for architecture and planning at Barcelona's Olympic Village.
Gold Medal for artistic merit awarded in 1997 by the city of Barcelona.

PAU, LLUIS

Born in 1950 in Castellfollit de la Roca, Spain.
Studied design at Eina de Barcelona (1968).
In 1969 and 1970 member of the jury of FAD (Fomentos Artes Decorativas), for architecture and interior architecture.
In 1971-1973, in Banyoles, founded with other artists the group TINT-1, later followed by TINT-2, in 1974 (setting up exhibitions and events).
Partner in 1973 of architects Martorell, Bohigas and Mackay, of the Barcelona agency Interiors Disseny, renamed at this time "IDP."
From 1976 to 1983, then from 1985 to1990, was involved in various cpacities in the direction of FAD, ADI-FAD (design section) and INFAD (interior architecture section).

Teaches design at Eina school, and gives many courses and lectures on signage and language exposition as a new experimental discipline (since 1994).

Principal realizations of IDP: in Barcelona, many offices, agencies, residential buildings; also shops: Aksa and La Tenda Animacio, shopping galleries Palau Nou de la Rambla, clinic of the Mutualidad Catalana, hotel Melia Sol; elsewhere in Spain, in Banyoles, municipal theater, café-bar 1929 and furniture shop Addicional; in Lloret de Mar, museum and cultural center of Can Garriga; in Palma de Majorca, boutique Intersport and villa Escarrer...

KING-MIRANDA ASSOCIATI

KING, PERRY

Born in 1938 in London.
Studied at Birmingham School of Art.
Set up in Italy in 1964, beginning of a long collaboration with Olivetti.
In 1975 went into partnership with Santiago Miranda in Milan.
In 1990 King & Miranda created EDEN (European Designers Network), with BRS Premsela Vonk in Amsterdam, MetaDesign in Berlin and Eleven Design in Copenhague.
Member of the University of Central England.

MIRANDA, SANTIAGO

Born in 1947 in Seville.
Studied in Seville.
In 1971 settled in Milan. In 1975 opened his agency with Perry King.
Member of the scientific committee of the Instituto Europeo di Disegno in Madrid.

Principal realizations:
Design: lamps Jill (1977), Aurora (1982), Aloa (1990), Aries (1993) for Arteluce, chair Vestita (1989) and office chair Air Mail (1984-1990) for Marcatré, chair Solea (1990) for Andrea World, chair De Triana (1992) for Atelier International/Vecta, portable telephone for Ericsson Mobile Communication (1995), AEDP prize, Madrid 1997.
Architecture: Interdecor showrooms in Tokyo (1989) and Sapporo (1990), Marcatré showrooms in London (1985-1986), Bologna (1986-1987), Paris (1989) and Madrid (1991), offices for Nuova Assicuratrice in Milan (1989), showrooms for Applicazioni (1993), Olimpia Splendid (1994) and Elettroplasticva (1996),

NARDI, CLAUDIO

Italian architect and designer Claudio Nardi has designed models for shops and brands Dolce & Gabbana, D&C, Gieffeffe Gianfranco Ferré, Ferré Jeans and Exté.

Principal realizations:
Architecture: in Italy, private homes, villas and apartments in Altamura, Arezzo, Florence, Formia, Lignano Sabbiadoro, Milan and Ravenna, shops Luisa Via Roma and BP Studio in Florence, boutiques Brana in Bari and Sbaiz in Lignano Sabbiadoro, offices, showroom and boutique Dolce & Gabbana in Milan, hotel Leonardo Da Vinci in Florence; renovation of apartments in Paris and London; commercial complexes in Koweït and Dubai.
Interior architecture: in Florence, showroom Exté, bar Apollo, boutiques Allegri, Silvana, San Francisco Story, Raspini and Desmo; boutiques Dantone, Desmo Via della Spiga and Valentino à Milan, Nick & Sons in Ravenna, Gente and Eleonora in Rome, Maison Des Toiles à Fukuoka (Japan), Atil Kutoglu in Vienna...

NEELAND, TORSTEN

Born in 1963 in Hamburg.
Studied design at the University of Hamburg.
Realizations: boutiques Uta Rausch in Düsseldorf, Ocky's in Hamburg. Designer objects sold in Hamburg, Milan, Munich and New York.

PEREGALLI, MAURIZIO

Born in 1951 in Varese, Italy.
Made his reputation by decorating the stores of Fiorucci and the chain Primavera, then by designing Giorgio Armani shops in Milan, London and New York, for which he created a standard furnishing system.
In 1984 he founded the Zeus Gallery in Milan, Via Vegevano, with Roberto and Walter Marcatti, Davide Mercatali and Ruben Mochi. For large-scale production they were joined by Iavicoli & Rossi, Claudio Nardi, Martin Skekely...

Objects of design: lamp Mura (1986), chair Glasnost (1988), office lamp Ventosa (1989), mannequins Cavaliere (1989), armchair Poltroncina for Armani (produced by Zeus)...

PHILIPPI, PATRICK

Born in 1940.
Realizations: Museum of Modern Art in Strasbourg (with Arata Isozaki), Polytechnic School of Strasbourg (with Oswald M. Ungers).

SAMSÓ, EDUARD

Born in Barcelona in 1956.
Graduated from the UETSAV—Escola Tecnica Superior d'Arquitectura del Vallès—(1973-1980).
In 1983 founded Samsó + Associates.
President of INFAD, interior architecture section of FAD (1985-1987), and vice-president of ADIFAD, industrial design section (1991-1993).
Professor at School of Design Eina (1987-1989), and visiting professor of ETSAB (1993-1995).
Grand prize FAD for best interior architecture (1987), EDIM prize (Madrid, 1988), medal of merit Santiaga Marco (1996).
Realizations:
Objects of design and furniture of Producción Contempóranea, B.D. Ediciones de Diseno, Carlos Jané, Driade and Nani Marquina.
Architecture: in Barcelona, hair-dressing salon Marcel (shopping gallery bd Rosa, 1987), fashion boutique Lurdes Bergada (Avinguda Diagonal, 1989), boutique The End, Calle de la Cruz, in Ibiza (1990)...

SIPEK, BOREK

Born in 1949 à Prague.
Studied furniture design at the School of Arts and Crafts in Prague (1964-1968), then architecture at the University School of Fine Arts in Hamburg (1969), and philosophy in Stuttgart (1973).
Graduated from the Technical University in Delft (1979).
In 1983 settled in Amsterdam, where he opened an architecture and design office.
Professor of architecture at the Academy of Applied Arts, Prague (1990).
Prizes Kho Liang Ie (1989) and Prins Bernhard Fond (1993), Chevalier des Arts and des Lettres (1991).

Individual exhibitions: Museum of Decorative Arts in Lyon (1987), Stedeljik Museum in Amsterdam (1991), Vitra Design Museum in Weil am Rhein, Germany (1992), Museum of Decorative Arts in Prague (1993).

Furniture and objects produced: in Italy, by Cleto Munari, Driade Spa, Maletti Spa, Sawaya & Moroni and Scarabas, in Austria by Leitner and Wittmann, in Switzerland by Vitra, in France by les Porcelaines de Sèvres and Bernardaud, in Germany by Anthologie Quartett and Süssmuth, in the Netherlands by Alterego, Mosa and Steltman Gallery Amsterdam-New York, and by Ajeto, in the Czech Republic.
Principal realizations in architecture:
Museum Het Kruithuis in Den Bosch, Netherlands (1993-1998), Kyoto Opera House (1994), Karl Lagerfeld boutique in Paris (1995), private homes in the Netherlands and Germany (1993-1997), 62 apartments for the municipality of Apeldoorn, Netherlands (1994-1996), boutique Shoebaloo in Rotterdam (1995), shop front for Komatsu in Tokyo (1996).

STUDIO GRANDA

HAROARDOTTIR, MARGRET

Born in 1959 in Reykjavik, Iceland.
Graduated from the Architectural Association of London (1984).
With Steve Christer, founded Studio Granda in Reykjavik in 1987.
Vice-president of the Association of Icelandic Architects (1993-1995).
Tutor at the Architectural Association of London (1994-1995).

CHRISTER, STEVE

Born in 1960 in Blackfyne, U.K.
Graduated from the Architectural Association of London (1984).
Co-director of the architecture workshop Rafha in Iceland (1992).
Visiting professor at Berlage Institute of Amsterdam (1994).
Tutor at Architectural Association of London (1994-1995).

Principal realizations: in Reykjavik, city hall (1988-1992), courthouse (1994-1996), fashion shops Eva Company (1994) and Galleri (1996), Modern Art Museum (first in competition, 1997); residential buildings in Iceland, Pingas in Reykjavik, Gardabae (1996), Seltjarnarnes (1997) and Kopavogur (1997); residence Aktion Poliphile in Wiesbaden, with Ressel & Partner (1990-1992).

UCHIDA, SHIGERU

Born in 1943 in Yokohama, Japan.
Graduated from Kuwasawa Design School in Tokyo (1966).
In 1970 opened his agency.
Lectured at Kuwasawa School (1973-) and University of Art and Design in Tokyo (1974-1978).
In 1981 founded Studio 80 with Toru Nishioka.
Japan Interior Designer's Association Award (1981), Mainichi prize (1987), special prize for best shop of the year (1990), Grand Prize Shokankyo 90 (1990).
Has lectured at American universities (Columbia, Parsons School of Design in 1986), Domus Academy (1992), Politecnicode Milan (1995), Dutch Center of Utrecht (1996).

Principal realizations:
Design: Free-Form-Chair (1969), chairs September (1977), Nirvana (1981), Ny Chair II (1986), lamp Tenderly (1985), watches Dear Morris and Dear Vera (1989)...
Architecture: in Tokyo, shops Scibu (1975-1980) and Tobu (1992), boutiques Issey Miyake (1976-1982) and Yohji Yamamoto (1983-1986), manicure parlor Longleage in

Hiroo (1997), bar Le Club in Roppongi (1986), restaurants Yuzutei in Nishiazabu (1986) and La Ranarita in Azumabashi (1991); hotels Il Palazzo in Fukuoka (1989) and Lobby in Kyoto (1994); tea rooms Ji-An, Gyo-an & So-An (1993), Fashion Museum of the city of Kobé (1997).

VÉRET, JEAN-LOUIS

Born in 1927 in Paris.
Based in Montrouge.
Graduated from the Ecole Nationale Supérieure des Beaux-Arts de Paris (1952).
From 1952 to 1955, collaborator of Le Corbusier in Paris, then in Ahmedabad (India).
Founder with Jean Renaudie, Pierre Riboulet and Gérard Thurnauer, of the "Atelier d'Architecture de Montrouge," created in 1958 and disbanded in 1978. Among other projects, the Atelier was responsible for: the holiday village Merlier at Cap-Camarat (1958-1965), a children's library, Cité de la Plaine, Clamart (1965), EDF buildings at Issy-les-Moulineaux (1961-1963) and Ivry-sur-Seine (1964-1967).
In 1959-1960, received a scholarship to study for a year at Harvard's Graduate School of Design offered by the Harkness Foundation. Toured the United States.
In 1968 named architect-in-chief of bâtiments civils and palais nationaux.
In 1984-85, commissaire général of the architecture section for "India Year" in France.
In 1985, published Architectures en Inde at Editions Electa Le Moniteur, Paris.
Since 1985 has worked closely with Mr. Shu Uemura.
Visiting critic at the Architecture School of Harvard University (1977-1978), visiting professor at the Architecture School in Nancy (1981). Taught at the École d'architecture de Paris-La Villette UP6 (1985-1993).
Prize of the Cercle d'Etudes architecturales (1965), officer of Arts and Letters, national Grand Prize in architecture 1981.
Medal of the city of Paris for the Shu Uemura boutique, Bd Saint-Germain (1987).

Realizations for Shu Uemura:
in Paris, design for the main offices and Bd Saint-Germain shop (1985-1986, and 1997-1998), Space Shu Uemura at Galeries Lafayette Haussmann (1990); Spaces Shu Uemura at Harvey Nichols in London (1991), Magna Plaza in Amsterdam (1993), shops in Grenoble and Strasbourg (1994).
In progress: a laboratory and workshop center for the manufacture of cosmetics in Sukumo-Shikoku, Japan.

Bibliography

Josep Maria Montaner, *Barcelone, la ville et son architecture,* Benedikt Taschen, 1997.

Beauty Salons & Fashion Boutiques, Shop Design Series, Editions Shotenkenchiku-Sha, Tokyo, 1994.

Brigitte Fitoussi, *Boutiques*, Editions du Moniteur, Electa, 1988.

Commercial Spaces, European Masters/3, Atrium, 1991.

Martin M. Pegler, *Stores*, Lifestyle, PBC International, New York, 1996.

François Fauconnet, Brigitte Fitoussi and Karin Leopold, *Vitrines d'architecture, les boutiques à Paris*, ed. Picard/ Pavillon de l'Arsenal, Paris, 1997.

World Shops & Fashion Boutiques, Shop Design Series, Editions Shotenkenchiku-Sha, Tokyo.

Achille Castiglioni, Ferrari P., Milan, 1984.

Mario Bellini, architecture, Ranzani E., Milan, 1988.

Guidot R. and Boissière O., *Ron Arad*, Paris, Editions Dis Voir, 1998.

Wolfgang Amsoneit, *Contemporary European Architects*, Benedikt Taschen, 1994.

Photo credits

Pages 140 to 149: Gabriele Basilico
Pages 122 to 129: Friederich Busam & Christoph Kicherer
Pages 40 to 45: Mario Ciampi
Pages 16 to 21: Abramo Conti
Pages 150 to 157: Dan Forer
Pages 66 to 73: Klaus Frahm
Pages 94 to 103: Josep Gri
Front cover, pages 74 to 81: Léon Gulikers
Pages 22 to 29: Joan Mundó
Pages 82 to 87, 88 to 93 and back cover: Nacása & Partners Inc.
Pages 46 to 53: Jordi Sarrto
Pages 8 to 15: Deidi von Schaewen
Pages 54 to 59, 60 to 65: Sigurgeir Sigurjónsson
Pages 114 to 121: Y. Takasa/Cretoria
Pages 30 to 39: Francesc Tur
Pages 130 to 139: David Williams
Pages 104 to 113: Andrea Zani

Printed in Italy